W9-BEO-700

NEW LEFT REVIEW 124

SECOND SERIES

JULY AUGUST 2020

PROGRAMME NOTES

SIMON HAMMOND: Knight's Moves

A retrospective on the life and work of pioneering cultural critic, theorist and practitioner Peter Wollen. From Methodist roots to Parisian exile, radical journalism to avant-garde filmmaking, auteurism and semiotics to the landmark *Raiding the Icebox*.

LOLA SEATON: Painting Nationalism Green?

If climate change were framed as a threat to the security of Western states, could it rally the electoral forces of the right to an environmentalist agenda? The eco-nationalist programme of Anatol Lieven anatomized in the latest instalment of NLR's green-strategy debate.

GÖRAN THERBORN: Global Middle Classes

A survey of new shifts within the world's vast 'in-between' classes and their contrasting trajectories in North and South. How should their theorization—or ideologization?—by development economists and financial journalists be read?

GAVIN RAE: Poland's Mirror to the West

Poland's Atlanticist friends, deeply involved in the country's de-communization, now look on in horror as the national-conservative right consolidates its rule, reaching for explanations in cultural stereotypes and the *trahison des clercs*. Gavin Rae recommends some self-critical reflection.

ALICE BAMFORD: Mathematics and Modern Literature

If modernist literature has been fascinated by the possibilities of mathematical formalism, mathematicians have repaid the compliment in their use of that paramount avant-garde form: the manifesto. Here we publish extracts from Alice Bamford's bravura treatment of experimentation at Bourbaki and Oulipo.

FRANCO MORETTI: The Roads to Rome

Twenty years after 'Conjectures on World Literature', Franco Moretti reassesses the research methodologies of close and distant reading in literary studies. Interpretation and measurement, history and textuality, struggle and discovery—how practicable a synthesis of their approaches?

BOOK REVIEWS

ALPA SHAH on K. S. Komireddi, *Malevolent Republic*. A polemic against the corruptions of India's once-hegemonic Congress Party, charged with paving the way for Hindutva's rise.

NICK BURNS on Yoram Hazony, *The Virtue of Nationalism*. An Israeli conservative defends the differentials of national states against the universalizing ethic of US and EU imperialism.

OLIVER EAGLETON on Keir Milburn, *Generation Left*. Age as the key modality of class, theorized by way of Hungarian sociology, autonomist Marxism and Badiouian philosophy.

CONTRIBUTORS

NICK BURNS: *studies intellectual history at Queen Mary University of London*

SIMON HAMMOND: *teaches in literature at* UCL; *see also* NLR *118*

GÖRAN THERBORN: *Professor Emeritus of sociology at Cambridge; his new book,* Inequality and the Labyrinths of Democracy, *will be published by Verso in 2020*

FRANCO MORETTI: *most recent book,* Far Country: Scenes from American Culture *(2019)*

GAVIN RAE: *teaches social science at Kozminski University, Warsaw; author of* Poland's Return to Capitalism *(2012) and* Privatising Capital *(2015)*

ALPA SHAH: *author of* Nightmarch *(2018) and* In the Shadows of the State *(2010); teaches anthropology at the* LSE

SIMON HAMMOND

KNIGHT'S MOVES

Peter Wollen

P ETER WOLLEN DIED in December last year in West Sussex, having lived with Alzheimer's for seventeen years.[1] Prior to this long winter, as writer, theorist, director, curator and editor, he was a heroic figure of the intellectual counterculture in Britain. His career followed a sinuous path. Viktor Shklovsky's image of the 'knight's move', often invoked by Wollen to describe the oblique, unpredictable advance of the avant-garde, could well be applied to his biography. A prime mover of journals, institutions and collectives throughout his life, NLR among them, he is perhaps best remembered as a pioneer of *auteur* criticism and film theory, a co-director of experimental films and an importer of intellectual ferment. An avant-gardist disdain for the division of art and politics, theory and practice, was also discernible at a lower register in Wollen's flouting of disciplinary and professional boundaries, in his conception of his multifarious work ('I don't see my books or my lectures as separate activities from my screen-writing or my film-making').[2] As a writer, he was by disposition an essayist, the six books he published, beginning with *Signs and Meaning in the Cinema* (1969), all to some degree assemblages. His oeuvre, which ranges across the artistic and intellectual life of the twentieth century, resembles an archipelago rather than a continent.

Such a nomadic orientation may in part be accounted for by family background. Wollen was born in 1938, in the London suburb of Walthamstow, into a socialist, pacifist household. His father was a Methodist minister and the family lived a committed, peripatetic life, moving every few years to a new parish as the job required.[3] Later writings register a few lasting memories of these years: the bombs falling during the Blitz, a visit to the Festival of Britain in the war's aftermath, a formative first film experience, the dazzling world of Bosch's *Garden of Earthly Delights* in his father's Phaidon library. Attitudes to money, possessions, roots were all assimilated by the oldest son. Spending much of his working life without stable income or headquarters, Wollen was unusually footloose, readily turning himself to new endeavours and phases of life. Such an inheritance was however tempered by a more libertine spirit. Rejecting religion wholesale, Wollen absorbed the household's political affiliations and aesthetic interests in his own fashion. He read prodigiously in the library of his Methodist boarding school, working his way through the shelves; a revelatory encounter with Kropotkin's *Memoirs of a Revolutionist* provided a cosmopolitan contrast to low-church socialism. Here, too, nascent enthusiasm for Dada, surrealism, existentialism, developed. A school report warning that the boy was 'in danger of becoming an intellectual' first gave him the idea that this was what he wished to be.[4]

In 1956, a scholarship took him to Oxford, where he studied English Literature at Christ Church.[5] Wollen, however, recalled learning more from his milieu than any official education; he was known as a poet and moved in a beatnik-inclined crowd. Intellectually, his attention was captured by what was happening in Paris—a friend, Patrick Bauchau, had brought back copies of *Cahiers du Cinéma*. Amongst the spires and quads, the iconoclasm of the critics gathered around André Bazin's journal (Godard, Rivette, Chabrol, Rohmer, Truffaut)—who championed Hollywood directors of westerns and gangster films as *auteurs*, their stature equal to the great shades of art and literature—had an electrifying effect. Years later, describing the critical outlook this fostered, Wollen drew a sharp contrast with his immediate forebears in English criticism, Raymond Williams and Richard Hoggart, both for their conception of culture as the way of life of a community, and the apprehension that in Britain's case this was threatened by the influx of American

---

[1] My profound thanks to Leslie Dick and Laura Mulvey.
[2] Peter Wollen, 'An Alphabet of Cinema', NLR 12, Nov–Dec 2001, p. 122. Collected in *Paris Hollywood: Writings on Film*, London and New York 2002.
[3] Douglas Wollen gave an account of his life as a minister in Ronald Fraser, ed., *Work*, Volume 2, London 1969.
[4] 'Interview with Serge Guilbaut and Scott Watson', *Last Call*, vol. 1, no. 3, Spring 2002.
[5] One of his tutors was J. I. M. Stewart, a scholar of modern literature and prolific detective novelist under the pen name Michael Innes.

mass culture.[6] By contrast, as a critic Wollen was engaged with art and aesthetics rather than culture in any more holistic sense, something that was only emboldened by the productions of Hollywood. From his vantage point British culture was stultifying, and in need of invigoration from beyond its shores.

On the run

Wollen was unconcerned with Oxbridge rankings and scraped through his Finals with a third-class degree. Eng. Lit. turned out not to be a passion; he wrote his Milton paper on Elvis Presley. Caught by National Service conscription just before it ended, he made a botched attempt to qualify as a conscientious objector. Refusing officer status out of solidarity, Wollen cut an isolated figure, and soon absconded from his barracks. As the sixties dawned, Wollen therefore found himself in a precarious situation—poor qualifications, no immediate prospects nor resources to fall back on, non-conformist by temperament, and on the run from the military police.

Where else but Paris? By his arrival in August 1959, the Young Turks of *Cahiers* were having their first directorial triumphs. Wollen recalled going to see Godard's *À bout de souffle* every day the week it came out in March 1960, captivated by its worship and desecration of cinematic tradition, by its collision of B-movies and modernism which made it seem 'as if you could love both of them at the same time'.[7] Habitué of the Beat Hotel, Wollen worked at Le Mistral bookshop to pay his way. In the screening rooms of the Cinémathèque Française, where the *nouvelle vague* had gained their own cinematic education, he began to develop 'from cultist to critic to theorist'.[8] Two other cinephiles, Eugene Archer and Andrew Sarris—several years Wollen's senior and already making their way as film critics in New York—also made pilgrimages to the Left Bank during this period. The trio would be instrumental to

---

[6] Hoggart bemoaned the effects of American mass culture, personified by the milk bar, in *The Uses of Literacy* (1957). Williams, while pioneering the study of popular forms, generally steered clear of the productions of Hollywood.

[7] 'JLG', *Paris Hollywood*, p. 74.

[8] 'Who the hell is Howard Hawks?', *Paris Hollywood*, p. 61. Wollen would allude to the significance of 'the magnificent Paris Cinémathèque' in *Signs and Meaning in the Cinema*, London [1998] 2013, expanded edition, p. 86.

disseminating the ethos of the *politique des auteurs* throughout the anglo-phone world.[9] Wollen retained a fidelity to this formation, his 'obsessive love' for classic Hollywood undiminished by later avant-garde commit-ments (in this regard he followed a similar path to Godard). 'I am still an auteurist. I still give priority to the avant-garde', he insisted in 1997.[10] The distance was not as vast as it might appear: auteurism could be con-sidered 'the last of a series of twentieth-century critical revolutions in the name of "modernism" and against the *ancien régime* of artistic values'.[11] The wider backdrop to Wollen's intellectual formation was, in fact, the afterglow of modernism in the post-war period, which saw its flourish-ing in the cinema, and a last round of avant-garde activity.

Wollen returned to London every so often, moving in a countercultural milieu. He shared a flat in Westbourne Terrace with the future founder of the underground newspaper *International Times*, John 'Hoppy' Hopkins; when he left, his room was taken by Barry Miles, another *IT* editor and founder of the Indica gallery and bookshop. Soon though, Wollen departed again. A friend from Oxford, David Sladen, now an edi-tor of the literary journal *New Departures*, was driving a jeep across the Continent to Iran and in need of a companion. With little to keep him in London, Wollen readily agreed to join. The motivation was to transport clandestine propaganda to the political opposition to the Shah. Finally reaching Tehran in the winter of 1960, having almost died from food poi-soning in Turkey, Wollen settled for several months in Pich-e Shemiran, absorbing the city's history, architecture and literature—he was struck to find the avenues named after poets—while teaching English at a teacher-training college. The western-backed coup against Mosaddegh had been followed by a prolonged period of repression in Iran. Wollen's time there coincided with a period of instability, with the removal of one prime minister and the installation of another, accompanied by bouts of unrest and state violence. Witnessing this had an 'important political effect', and was an immediate impetus for his emergence as a writer.[12] Back in London, he was asked by the recently installed editors of NLR,

[9] Andrew Sarris's 'Notes on the Auteur Theory in 1962', credited with first translat-ing *Cahiers's* doctrine into English, ran in a special issue of *Film Culture* (no. 27, Winter 1962–63) devised by Sarris and Eugene Archer, also a friend of Bauchau. Wollen was close to Archer in Paris, but did not get to know Sarris until later.
[10] 'Lee Russell Interviews Peter Wollen' [1997], in *Signs and Meaning*, respectively p. 237, p. 218.
[11] 'The Canon', *Paris Hollywood*, p. 218.
[12] Interview, 'From Cinephilia to Film Studies', in Lee Grieveson and Haidee Wasson, eds, *Inventing Film Studies*, Durham and London 2008, p. 224.

with whom he had been partially acquainted at Oxford, to contribute an essay about the country—the first of the Third World surveys that would become a signature of the journal.

Still fearing detection by the military police, Wollen wrote under the *nom de plume* Lucien Rey.[13] 'Persia in Perspective' was a panoptic survey in two parts, published sequentially in the first half of 1963: spanning geography, development and social composition, it provided a *longue durée* account of the country's history. The distinguishing features of Wollen's prose style are already apparent here: spare, precise, authoritative, averse to rhetoric, formal in its way, but punctuated by flashes of imagery, aphorism, the sudden pressure of feeling or personal inflection. What emerges from his portrait is a country of 'startling contrasts and anomalies—juxtapositions of new and old, foreign and local, urban and rural, sedentary and nomadic', whose 'tensions and contradictions' primarily stem from 'the deforming impact of imperialism'.[14] The emotional connection wrought by his experiences is most evident in the diagnosis of the present moment: while 'an army of political apologists, ghost-writers and well-paid liars' outside Iran paint the Shah as a dynamic and progressive ruler, the 'squalor and fear' in which his people live is never mentioned. Though no immediate change was in sight, Wollen foresaw the regime facing a growing challenge; a postscript recorded a renewed wave of popular uprisings. Further pieces by Lucien Rey contributed to the journal's global coverage of revolution and counter-revolution. After Iran, Wollen assessed the future prospects of the revolution in Zanzibar—initially 'the brightest spark in Africa'—following its integration with mainland Tanganyika. Later, he wrote on the massacres of the communists in Indonesia, drawing on reports gathered by Benedict Anderson and Ruth McVey to produce an account of the events that precipitated the extermination of the party.[15]

At the movies

Alongside his political writings, Wollen played a prominent role in setting the journal's cultural tempo. He became an editor of the new 'Motifs'

---

[13] The alias was devised by NLR editor Roger Murray, intended to be of suitably ambiguous nationality, definitely not British. Lucien Goldmann and Fernando Rey may have provided subliminal inspiration.
[14] 'Persia in Perspective—I', NLR 1/19, Mar–Apr 1963, pp. 39, 41.
[15] 'The Revolution in Zanzibar', NLR 1/25, May–June 1964, p. 29; 'Dossier of the Indonesian Drama', NLR 1/36, March–April 1966.

section, whose first instalment at the start of 1964 presented studies of the composer John Cage, the pianist Cecil Taylor and—Wollen's own contribution—the B-movie director Samuel Fuller. Wollen also wrote short reviews of novels, works of criticism and history (under the initials L. R.), the first of which argued that the latest work of Burroughs demanded reading despite the depths of its nihilism. Amongst Wollen's editorial achievements was introducing a range of writers from other countries—including the Iranian modernist Sadegh Hedayat and the Italian poet Franco Fortini. The latter Wollen applauded for his navigation of artistic and political commitment in an age when 'the poet is trapped between epitaphs and manifestos'; the aim instead was to construct a poetic culture from the 'fragmentary inheritance' of revolution that survived the Stalinist period, the legacy of the surrealist and 'social realist' currents and, most importantly, of 'internal *emigré*' poets such as Brecht, József, Hikmet, Zukovsky.[16] His own, later, excavations of the avant-garde would be conducted in similar spirit.

The most celebrated contributions were his pieces on film, the first fruits of a gleefully excessive cinephilia: during this time Wollen was going to between ten and twenty films a week, criss-crossing the city to backstreet and outlying repertory theatres, ticking them off in his copy of *Vingt ans de Cinéma Américain*.[17] The procedures and affinities of auteurism encouraged a spirit of completism; years later, Wollen would define cinephilia as 'an obsessive infatuation with film, to the point of letting it dominate your life'.[18] One companion on these excursions was the equally cinephiliac Laura Mulvey, recently graduated from Oxford, whom Wollen met through university friends in the spring of 1963. Between 1964 and 1967, under his second alias, Lee Russell, Wollen produced a series of profiles of directors, spanning American and European cinema.[19] These were prefaced by an agenda-setting broadside against *The Contemporary Cinema* by Penelope Houston, then editor of *Sight & Sound*. The magazine, funded by the British Film Institute, was the dominant force in British film criticism, its writers also holding court in the national

[16] 'Franco Fortini', NLR 1/38, July–Aug 1966, p. 80.
[17] Jean-Pierre Coursodon and Yves Boisset, *Vingt ans de Cinéma Américain*, Paris 1961.
[18] 'An Alphabet of Cinema', p. 119.
[19] Of this alias: 'Lee, that was one of the pen-names William Burroughs had used—right? William Lee! Russell probably came from Bertrand Russell. I don't know, something like that!'. See 'Interview with Guilbaut and Watson', 2001.

newspapers and magazines. For Wollen and his co-thinkers, it had come to embody a staid orthodoxy. The review presented Houston's book as an exemplification of these deficiencies, charging it with cultural snobbery, impressionist relativism, paucity of method, no interest in style, amongst other charges—it demonstrated, he writes, what remains to be achieved in film criticism in Britain, and the futility of attempting this 'unarmed with any methodology or serious ideological or aesthetic purpose'.[20]

The eleven directorial studies that followed—laconic works of auteur criticism appearing like a series of fireworks—were Wollen's first contribution to addressing this. They sparkle with vivid argumentation. Naturally, they took their template from *Cahiers*, but while delineating each distinctive style, the emphasis falls upon the director's world-view, in a diagnostic approach that Wollen credited to the work of Lucien Goldmann, particularly his study of the novels of André Malraux in *Pour une sociologie du roman* (1964). (Fuller portrays an America riven by violence and teetering into lunacy, which he attempts to redeem with an overflow of 'romantic nationalism'; Renoir is pledged to the humanism of the 'ordinary man' and the simple life, leading to a flight in his films to society's margins, and from public to private.[21]) While distinguishing original attributes, integral motifs and preoccupations, celebrating artistry and conceptual richness, the series did not shirk from outlining shortcomings. Cinema critics 'must be ruthless', he insisted—Sternberg's aristocratic aloofness can render his films 'blind and ludicrous', Ford can be faulted for 'his many reactionary attitudes, his sentimentalism, his lapses into childishness'.[22] Stress falls on narrowness of perspective or flaws of vision, tensions and antagonisms of various kinds.

The most significant criticisms, perhaps, come in Wollen's treatment of Godard, whose films up until then, he argued, were marked by 'the

---

[20] 'Culture and Cinema', NLR 1/21, Oct 1963, p. 115. Houston, who became editor of *Sight & Sound* in 1956, was a key figure of the previous generation of British film enthusiasts. Attending Oxford a decade earlier, she had been an editor of *Sequence*, the film magazine out of which grew the 'Free Cinema' movement of Lindsay Anderson, Karel Reisz, Tony Richardson and Lorenza Mazzetti.

[21] 'Jean Renoir', NLR 1/25, May–June 1964, p. 57; 'Samuel Fuller', NLR 1/23, Jan–Feb 1964, p. 89.

[22] For ruthlessness, see 'Howard Hawks', NLR 1/24, Mar–Apr 1964, p. 85; 'Josef von Sternberg', NLR 1/36, Mar–Apr 1966, p. 81; 'John Ford', NLR 1/29, Jan–Feb 1965, p. 73.

absence of politics', a void which condemns them to 'rootlessness and despair', where 'nothing remains except the scattered, expendable efforts of artists and romantics'.[23] Beyond shared political commitments, there was an evident affinity between Wollen's enterprise and the wider project of NLR, which during the sixties committed itself to a thoroughgoing critical re-evaluation of British history and culture, and a concerted turn to the intellectual life of the continent. Wollen later joked of its 'national nihilist' streak.[24] His parallel project entailed the same turn away from national culture; for him, Hollywood refracted through French theory—both anathema to respectable opinion—would help provide an antidote to British provincialism.

During this time, Wollen spent a year in Italy working for the *International Socialist Journal*. Founded at the start of 1964, the journal was led by Lelio Basso, a senior figure on the left of Italy's Socialist Party. Published in both English and French, it was intended to provide an international forum for exchange and collaboration. Wollen joined in the summer, living first in Milan, then Rome when the journal relocated its headquarters, working alongside a friend from university and NLR, Jon Halliday. In addition to editorial duties, under the guise of Lucien Rey, Wollen's beat was Britain at home and abroad. His first piece was about the unfolding situation in Aden, a remnant of Empire now racked by revolt. Later he turned his fire on the Wilson government, which at the onset of the sterling crisis had run cap in hand to the IMF, putting paid to its national plan. Wollen argued for public investment, workers' control and an end to overseas military expenditure ('Never again must Britain act as a world gendarme'), while criticizing Wilson's 'fundamentally inadequate palliatives' for the structural problems of the economy.[25]

This was also a period of possibility and capitulation for the parliamentary left in Italy. The PSI entered government for the first time in 1963,

---

[23] 'Reply to Robin Wood on Godard', NLR 1/39, Sept–Oct 1966, pp. 86, 87. Another auteurist critic, but one with a Leavisite constitution, Robin Wood, had recently argued in the journal's pages that Godard's films expressed a rejection of contemporary society in response to its discarding of cultural tradition; Wollen countered that Godard saw art as antagonistic, and society as nothing more than an instrument of violence.

[24] 'Lee Russell Interviews Peter Wollen', p. 243. Isaac Deutscher was the first to apply this term to NLR. See Perry Anderson, *English Questions*, London 1992, p. 5.

[25] 'Aden', *International Socialist Journal*, no. 5–6, Sep–Dec 1964, p. 610; 'Labour's First Budget', *ISJ*, no. 9, June 1965, p. 369.

as junior partners of the Christian Democrats. Hopes that parts of their programme could be achieved soon dissipated, and the left flank, Basso amongst them, broke away in protest, forming a splinter party in January 1964. Wollen contributed a report for NLR on the developing situation in early 1965, covering the protracted horse-trading of the presidential elections that had laid bare the dysfunction of the coalition and provided a symbolic victory for the left. He also made a brief return visit to Iran in 1965; there were plans to build his study of the country into a book. For the ISJ, he gauged the strength of the array of opposition forces, arguing that the current 'entr'acte must not be mistaken for the end of the drama', that the country's 'apparent somnolence' hid 'frustrated energies' which would in time find political expression and sweep away the current regime. For NLR, he reported on the fallout of an assassination attempt on the Shah, seeing little hope of a fair trial for the students opportunistically tied to it. Paying tribute to their steadfastness, he saw them as inaugurating a new phase of struggle.[26]

An uprising in film studies

Amid the ferment of the mid-sixties, Wollen was living hand-to-mouth: work for the Bertrand Russell Peace Foundation, a commission for a viability study of the Volta Dam, a first foray into screenwriting, when Eugene Archer enlisted him to adapt Faulkner's *Wild Palms*—a favourite of the *nouvelle vague*—in the hope, never realized, of selling it to Truffaut. Back in London, he was living with Mulvey in a large bohemian household in Ladbroke Grove, where their son Chad would be born in 1969. An invitation—on the strength of the Lee Russell pieces—to join the British Film Institute in 1966 transformed this situation. Wollen was one of a number of young cinephiles brought together by Paddy Whannel to run the BFI's Education Department. Whannel had recently co-written *The Popular Arts* (1964) with Stuart Hall, a pathbreaking contribution to the study of popular culture in all its forms as a subject of social importance; both would follow the ambition expressed in the book of creating an institutional base for taking this forward. Under Whannel's tenure, the BFI Education Department possessed a campaigning zeal, acting rather as a university department-in-waiting, running courses, seminars, and publishing research intended to promote film as a subject alongside the

---

[26] Respectively, 'The Italian Presidential Elections', NLR 1/30, Mar–Apr 1965; 'Iran Today—and Tomorrow?', ISJ, no. 9, June 1965, pp. 382, 388; 'Guilt by Association', NLR 1/35, Jan–Feb 1966.

other arts. 'In retrospect', Wollen later reflected, 'it all looks positively heroic in its optimism.'[27]

Amongst its activities was a series of seminars curated by Wollen, held at the BFI offices in Soho. In 'Towards a New Criticism?', written at this time, he set their intentions in the context of film's exclusion from the 'sacred groves' of the university—of forging an approach that reck-oned with the uniqueness of cinema as a medium and drew resources from nearby disciplines, particularly sociology, linguistics and semiot-ics.[28] This was a seminal moment for the diffusion of French theory in Britain: that same year, 1967, Frank Kermode ran a comparable seminar at University College London, visited by Barthes and Eco, credited with importing theory into English studies. Wollen also commissioned a series of books under the rubric 'Cinema One', many of which developed out of the seminars. These were for the most part author- or genre-oriented: studies of Hawks and Visconti, interviews with Pasolini and Sirk, books devoted to the western and the gangster film.[29] The series was a source of ongoing tension with the neighbouring BFI Publications Department, responsible for *Sight & Sound* and also headed by Penelope Houston. Wrangling led to it being published as a joint series, but without col-laboration behind the scenes; their respective books were published autonomously and evinced polar preoccupations.

Wollen's first book, *Signs and Meaning in the Cinema* (1969), was pub-lished as part of this gathering corpus. The most expressly theoretical of the set, he later described it as a 'contribution toward an uprising in film studies'.[30] Written at lightning speed in May 68, it reflected the sense of

---

[27] 'Lee Russell Interviews Peter Wollen', p. 211. See also the obituary for Paddy Whannel in *Screen*, signed by Wollen and others: *Screen*, Summer 1980, pp. 10–14.
[28] 'Towards a New Criticism?', *Screen Education*, Sept–Oct 1967, p. 90. *Working Papers on the Cinema*, London 1969, which collected papers delivered at the semi-nars, including Wollen's 'Cinema and Semiology: Some Points of Contact', gives a sense of these preliminary encounters.
[29] As editor of the 'Cinema One' series, Wollen insisted that the books should pro-ceed synchronically, rather than running in chronological order; they were also expected to make a theoretical contribution. See Richard Roud, *Godard* (1967), Geoffrey Nowell-Smith, *Luchino Visconti* (1968), Robin Wood, *Howard Hawks* (1968), Peter Graham, ed., *The New Wave* (1968), Oswald Stack, ed., *Pasolini on Pasolini* (1969), Jim Kitses, *Horizons West* (1969), Nicholas Garnham, *Samuel Fuller* (1971), Jon Halliday, *Sirk on Sirk* (1971), Alan Lovell, *Studies in Documentary* (1972), Colin McArthur, *Underworld U.S.A.* (1972), Andrew Tudor, *Theories of Film* (1974).
[30] '68/88: Thinking Theory', *Film Comment*, July 1988, p. 50.

the beginning of a new epoch and a break with the old: the upheavals of that year, Wollen later wrote, were 'a moment of exhilarating dreams', where it seemed possible to 'set off in startling new directions'. The book was 'full of the same sense of a beginning—a new approach to film studies, a new intellectual seriousness, new theoretical developments, the promise of a new cinema, even the foundation of a new academic discipline'.[31] Its introduction criticized both the marginal position of film in the study of aesthetics and the splendid isolation of anglophone film criticism. In contrast, the book was fuelled by new currents from France. He described himself as having been 'swept off my feet' by Barthes's foundational *Éléments de sémiologie*; Christian Metz's first foray into its application, 'Le Cinéma, Langue ou Langage?', also provided crucial stimulation, although his own position would be critical of both.[32] Theory, at this moment, appeared to be converging with practice, with developments in European cinema seeming to demand the application of semiology and structuralism.

Signs and Meaning proceeds in three sections. Eisenstein first of all provides an effective means of establishing the artistry, as well as the theoretical sophistication, of cinema. A reconstruction of Eisenstein's career—his formation as a filmmaker within the matrix of the revolution, his achievements tragically curtailed by the consolidation of Stalin's power—is set alongside the development of his ideas of montage, typage and synaesthesia, his dreams of a synthesis of art and science, of affect and idea, and eventual retreat to symbolism. The Russian avant-garde of the 1920s—'startlingly and breathtakingly original'—was an enduring inspiration.[33] Lodestar of the marriage of theory and practice, Wollen presented Eisenstein, contra Bazin, as the first and perhaps still the most important theorist of cinema.

Turning to auteurism, *Signs and Meaning* argued that it had yet to establish firm theoretical principles, and proposed structuralism as a potential solution. The methodology developed for the study of myth and folklore can, he argues, characterize the auteur by demonstrating a 'core of repeated motifs' as well as a 'system of differences and

[31] 'Lee Russell Interviews Peter Wollen', p. 211.
[32] 'Lee Russell Interviews Peter Wollen', p. 223. The texts by Barthes and Metz both appeared in the French journal *Communications* 4, 1964.
[33] *Signs and Meaning*, p. 4. For Wollen, Camilla Gray's *The Great Experiment: Russian Art 1863–1922*, London 1962, was an important introduction.

oppositions'.[34] In the case of Hawks, employed as test case, this structure of difference lay in the relation between his adventures and comedies, the latter upturning the value system of the former. Structuralism might also provide a system of evaluation: the more complex set of antino- mies in Ford's work lifted him above Hawks. The chapter exhibits both an anti-elitism—rejecting any condescension towards Hollywood—and also a kind of anti-populism, in insisting upon a rigorous theoreticism. While arguing for its efficacy, Wollen also presses up against the limits of the approach—auteurism is a system only for the analysis of a whole corpus; its exclusive focus on the director means that many features of the films must be dismissed as so much noise.

Finally, Wollen provided an overview of ongoing debates between Barthes, Metz, Eco, Pasolini and others about the language of film—of crucial importance, he writes, for without an understanding of the sys- tem of signs and how they produce meaning, criticism was condemned to 'massive imprecision and nebulosity'. Wollen's intervention was to propose the thinking of the American pragmatist C. S. Peirce and his taxonomy of icon, index and symbol, insisting that other proposals had essentially restricted themselves to only one of these aspects. But film language did not operate in the same way as verbal language and its analysis required a different set of tools. Peirce's model, rather than Saussure's, could better help explain the value of a director like Godard— now fully politicized—who had, by producing work that is 'an almost equal amalgam of the symbolic, the iconic and the indexical', come closest of all filmmakers to realizing cinema's semiotic possibilities, pro- ducing works of 'conceptual meaning, pictorial beauty and documentary truth.' The book ends with a renewed assault on the subsidiary position of film and its exclusion from the education system; in Wollen's depic- tion, it is a discipline in its infancy—'an enormous amount of work still remains to be done'.[35]

Signs and Meaning acted as a catalyst for the emerging field of film stud- ies, and later became a classic of the discipline. Vigorously debated by the new cohort of critics, the book's reception was sharply polarized, largely along generational lines. Within the BFI, opposition to the Education Department steadily intensified. Mulvey later recalled the 'near apo-

[34] *Signs and Meaning*, pp. 75, 77.
[35] *Signs and Meaning*, pp. 10, 132, 200.

plexy' that the admixture of theory and popular cinema provoked in the administration.[36] This occurred within a wider context of organizational turmoil, as calls came from within and beyond the BFI for democratization, re-organization, even wholesale replacement. The most determined challenge came in 1970, when an action committee, Wollen among their number, issued a manifesto calling for the dismissal of the governors and attempted to move against them at the annual general meeting.[37]

The calls for change were partly inspired by the example of the Cinémathèque, and indeed took place alongside parallel conflicts in Paris, where in an opening salvo of 68, protests had met the attempted removal of its fabled director, Henri Langlois. At the BFI, the culmination came the following year with a countermove by the governors. The Education Department, already distrusted for its research ambitions and cultural politics, was identified as the main source of internal trouble, and a review was commissioned to clip its wings. Whannel along with a group of his colleagues responded by tendering their resignations, bringing the golden age of the department to a close.[38] Though cut short, these years are celebrated for their pioneering contribution to the establishment of film studies as a discipline in Britain, and as a crucible for the development of film theory.

Wollen had, by this point, transferred his energies, working to renovate the journal *Screen* into an institution to carry their work forward. Formerly the house journal of the Society for Education in Film and Television, *Screen* was relaunched in Spring 1971 as, in Wollen's words, 'a militantly theoretical journal'.[39] Bringing together critics gathered around NLR with a grouping from Cambridge, it would become the supreme journal of film theory in English, with an outsize impact across the Anglosphere. It would also prove to be highly contentious, memorably accused of intellectual terrorism by one of its many adversaries.[40] A generation initially united in opposition to conservative opinion now

---

[36] Mulvey, 'From Cinephilia to Film Studies', *Inventing Film Studies*, p. 227.
[37] On this, see above all Geoffrey Nowell-Smith, 'The 1970 crisis at the BFI and its aftermath', *Screen*, Winter 2006.
[38] Whannel and his colleagues' resignation letter was published in *Screen*, Autumn 1971.
[39] Interview with Guilbaut and Watson, 2001.
[40] Andrew Britton, 'The Ideology of *Screen*', *Movie*, Winter 1978–79. For another view see Colin MacCabe, 'Class of 68', in *Theoretical Essays*, Manchester 1985.

fractured over questions of theory. Controversy was not limited to the journal's reception: its forays into psychoanalysis were met with a wave of resignations from the journal's board. Its early years saw the development of what is referred to in shorthand as 'Screen theory'—broadly, an amalgam of Marxism, feminism, semiotics and psychoanalysis, marshalled for ideological critique; Mulvey would publish 'Visual Pleasure and Narrative Cinema' in its pages.[41] In this regard, the journal was a counterpart of *Cahiers* in these years, which from strictly aesthetic beginnings had since become heavily theoretical and political, with both Althusser and Lacan looming large.

Wollen concurrently was involved in another journal, a cousin of NLR, the arresting weekly *Seven Days*, spearheaded by Alexander Cockburn for its short-lived run from 1971–72. Amongst his contributions, Wollen produced essays for its pages on ideas; notably writing expositions of the Oedipus complex and surrealism. The former would be the core concept of his films of the following decade; the latter an exemplar of the kind of avant-garde—politically oriented, retreating neither into formalism or functionalism—that he would champion. Elsewhere in the paper, two critical reviews demonstrated loyalties and aspirations: *The Last Picture Show* (1971), directed by the onetime fellow auteurist critic Peter Bogdanovich, was damned for its conservative recycling of elements of classic Hollywood, while a history of realism in the visual arts provided occasion to excoriate its limitations.

New avant-gardes

Wollen's thinking evolved dramatically in this period. A new conclusion to *Signs and Meaning*, written for a third edition published in 1972, signalled several developments. First, a decisive shift to avant-garde film, influenced by post-68 Godard and by North American Structural film: *Wavelength* by Michael Snow (1967) and *Zorn's Lemma* (1970) by Hollis Frampton most significantly. Accompanying this was a theoretical move towards post-structuralism, and from pedagogy to— incipiently—filmmaking. A change of mood is evident, from discussion of what cinema *is*, to what cinema *should be*. The book, he now reflected, had been written in the context of a reconnection of cinema with the

---

[41] *Screen*, Autumn 1975.

'modern movement' in the arts. The great breakthroughs of modernism had occurred when cinema was in its infancy, its impact was only briefly felt before being extinguished by authoritarianism. Now, however, it was possible to discern a new convergence. A variety of factors was responsible, not least new, affordable film-making technology; there was also a political stimulus—the first avant-gardes lifted by the winds of revolution, now the ferment of student revolt and liberation struggles. In particular, Wollen emphasized the semiological dimension of the modernist project—the disjunction it wrought between signifier and signified, its conception of the work as a text that is 'open rather than closed; multiple rather than single; productive rather than exhaustive'—ready now to be taken forward. Such a commitment necessarily cast the preceding book in a new light: the auteur is now relegated to an 'unconscious catalyst', while Hollywood becomes significant principally because it is in confrontation with it that the new can be produced.[42]

This sense of taking up the baton of the avant-garde was part of a wider moment of critical rediscovery. *Screen,* as one participant in this, published a range of discussions and translations, including documents from *Lef* and *Novy Lef,* with a view to assembling a genealogy of radical practice. Reflecting on the intellectual climate that had followed the Russian Revolution in *Signs and Meaning,* Wollen had noted that with 'the breakdown of the old academic system, there was not a slackening of intellectual pace, but actually an intensification. There was the crystallization of an authentic intelligentsia, rather than an academic hierarchy: like all intelligentsias, it was built around a revival of serious journalism and polemic. Literary theorists, such as Viktor Shklovsky in particular, issued manifestos, wrote broadsides, collaborated enthusiastically on magazines like *Lef*'.[43] There were certain parallels, of which its participants were fully conscious, with this lively period of little magazines produced by freewheeling intellectuals prior to film's academicization.

It was in this climate that Wollen produced a broader portrait of the currents and fortunes of the Russian avant-garde, 'Art in Revolution', published in 1971. In the immediate aftermath of the revolution, with

---

[42] *Signs and Meaning,* pp. 133, 140, 145. See also Fredric Jameson, 'Periodizing the 60s', *Social Text,* Spring–Summer, 1984.
[43] *Signs and Meaning,* p. 3.

the avant-garde in the ascendancy, two strands were given official sanction: on the one hand, the Cubist and Futurist avant-garde; on the other, the Proletkult grouping. Initially there was considerable overlap in their activities, but this was short-lived, for as Wollen outlined, they represented rather different tendencies—one of artists bringing their specialist skills to bear, the other claiming that the proletariat, having achieved political power, would produce its own art. At stake was the relation between the working class and a radical intelligentsia, a problematic that eventually prompted a turn to functionalism, in which art was subordinated to the exigencies of production. For Wollen, this discarded a sense of its semiotic and psychic capacities; his loyalty was with those who clung to art's visionary and imaginary potential. None of these tendencies, in any case, would emerge triumphant. Stalin's cultural policy called for a return to order; functionalism of a kind was retained but stripped of its futurism. Wollen concluded with the avant-garde vanquished, and a sombre vignette of Malevich's funeral, buried in a white coffin with a Suprematist black square above him, but with a prophecy of resurrection: 'One day all the white coffins will re-open and the phantoms will emerge to resume combat'.[44]

This historical commentary was produced with an eye fixed on the contemporary. A second key essay, 'Godard and Counter-Cinema', published in 1972, was more explicit, employing Godard's latest film, *Vent d'est* (1970), to lay out tenets for a radical film aesthetics. This was a time, Wollen wrote in retrospect, when he and others 'wrote drafts of guidelines for possible futures under the pretext of theorizing contemporary film practice, looking for alternative ways of filmmaking'.[45] Taking inspiration from Brecht's taxonomy of the distinctions between epic and naturalist theatre, Wollen proposed several features of contrast between orthodox and counter-cinema, between identification and estrangement, transparency and foregrounding. A criticism though is levelled against Godard's increasing suspicion of narrative and of fiction, Wollen countering that this is a simplification, as cinema cannot simply reveal truth, but instead produces meanings to be measured against other meanings. Heralding the film as a pioneering achievement, Wollen nevertheless insisted that it marked only the 'starting-point for work on a revolutionary cinema'.[46]

---

[44] *Readings and Writings: Semiotic Counter-Strategies*, London 1982, p. 78.
[45] 'Knight's Moves', *Camera Obscura, Camera Lucida: Essays in honour of Annette Michelson*, Amsterdam 2003, p. 147.
[46] *Readings and Writings*, p. 91.

Another landmark intervention in the discourse of radical film was 'The Two Avant-Gardes' of 1975.[47] Rather as Bazin had lamented a bifurcation in cinematic realism and expressed hopes of a rapprochement, in this essay, Wollen identifies one in avant-garde film—between a current represented by the Film-Makers' Cooperative movement in New York, home of Structural film, and the more expressly political work of Godard and Straub–Huillet in particular, centred around Paris. Despite points of contact, the two differed sharply, between essentially formalist and content-oriented strategies, as well as distinct modes of production, institutions and cultural positions. Wollen explained this as the product of the uneven development of modernism and film, arguing that the split first arose in the 1920s, between those like Léger and Moholy-Nagy who came to film from painting, and those such as Eisenstein and Vertov associated with theatre and poetry. Painting was uniquely amenable to an art of pure signifiers, and so this current in film has tended towards abstraction, while the other retained a concern with representation and narrative. Wollen's diagnosis is ultimately advocacy of a particular kind of film, one that forges a route between narrowly formalist or content-driven strategies. He concludes on a note of possibility—typical of his writing of the period—that film offers more opportunity than any other medium to take the project of the avant-garde forward.

Theorist-practitioners

This represented the declaration of a filmmaker as much as that of a critic or theorist. The previous year had seen the release of the first of his film collaborations with Mulvey. As both theorist and activist in the new women's liberation movement—she participated in the disruption of the 1970 Miss World competition at the Albert Hall—Mulvey produced a series of major essays bringing together film, feminism and psychoanalysis.[48] Their work now converged on the path pioneered by Eisenstein of combining theory and practice. In form and subject matter, their first films were intended to synthesize both wings of avant-garde film, and to forge an alliance between the avant-garde and the feminist politicization of the image. They can be situated within the blossoming of

---

[47] 'The Two Avant-Gardes', *Studio International*, November 1975; also collected in *Readings and Writings*.
[48] These include 'Fears, Fantasies and the Male Unconscious' (*Spare Rib*, 1973), 'Fassbinder and Sirk' (*Spare Rib*, 1974), 'Visual Pleasure and Narrative Cinema' (*Screen*, 1975) and 'Film, Feminism and the Avant-Garde' (1978), collected in *Visual and Other Pleasures*, London 1989.

experimental feminist film of the 1970s that includes the work of their friends Chantal Akerman and Yvonne Rainer.[49]

Their debut, *Penthesilea* (1974) was made during a stint at Northwestern University, at Whannel's invitation, using the department's equipment and Wollen's lecturer's salary for production funds. It takes Heinrich von Kleist's play of 1808, which reworked the gender roles of Penthesilea and Achilles, as a basis for a sharp, feature-length investigation of the Amazon myth, probing it as symbol of feminist resistance as well as inscription of male fears and fantasies. The film proceeds in five disaggregated sections, corresponding to the categories of theatre, verbal language—a roving lecture by Wollen—plastic arts, film and video. Emphasis falls on women's exclusion from the symbolic and the possibility of speaking within patriarchy; in Wollen's later description, this and their subsequent two films were 'symbolic quests in search of the place from which women could utter the repressed counter-meanings of patriarchal discourse'.[50]

Wollen undertook intermittent teaching throughout the period. After Northwestern, he took up a fellowship at Essex University, one of the first film positions in English universities. Sponsored by the BFI, this was an initiative of Whannel's that survived his departure.[51] Wollen characteristically chose to be stationed in the Linguistics Department, and alongside his teaching on film established a class on semiotics. That year he also had a major success as a screenwriter, with the release of Antonioni's *The Passenger* (1975), an existential thriller co-written with his friend Mark Peploe. The duo had collaborated on a number of scripts throughout the late sixties, but this was the first to catch wind when the screenplay was bought by Carlo Ponti. Antonioni, MGM and Jack Nicholson were a change of pace—Wollen joked that *Penthesilea* could have been made for the cost of the press party at Cannes—but it was his last venture of this kind; his attention was absorbed by experimental and theoretical film.[52]

---

[49] A model of directorial collaboration was also provided by Jean-Marie Straub and Danièle Huillet, whose first film, *Machorka–Muff*, was made in 1963.

[50] 'The Field of Language in Film', *October*, Summer 1981, p. 53.

[51] For an account of this posting, see Richard Dyer, 'The BFI Lectureships in Film', *Screen Education*, Summer 1976.

[52] 'Lee Russell Interviews Peter Wollen', p. 227; 'The Passenger', in *Time Out*, 4–10 July 1975, p. 9.

A radical film culture had by now developed in London, with a network of little magazines, a set of institutions including the London Film-Makers' Co-Op and Independent Filmmakers Association, with which Wollen was closely involved, and financial support from the BFI and the Arts Council. The highwater mark was the International Forum of Avant-Garde Film of 1976, which Wollen co-organized with the intention of fostering dialogue between the wings of the movement. In a reflection twenty years on, Wollen suggested that the convergence had been most successfully accomplished in Britain, where for a season avant-garde film established itself as a 'national force'.[53] A second Mulvey–Wollen feature film, *Riddles of the Sphinx* (1977) emerged from this atmosphere. Once again, the film brought avant-garde strategy to bear on myth, representation, language and patriarchy, here to address motherhood as both political and psychoanalytic category. Proceeding in sections, in this case expressly theoretical and symbolic elements are arranged around a central dramatic narrative told in thirteen 360-degree panning shots. The conceptual apparatus centres on the role of the Sphinx in the Oedipus myth, proposed as a representation of the place of the mother and the female unconscious in the symbolic order. Rather than merely a diagnosis, Wollen described the film as a 'challenge to Lacan's assumption that language is primarily a vehicle for the patriarchal Law, rather than for the matriarchal riddle'.[54] A short film, *Amy!* (1980), stands as a coda, interrogating the figure of the heroine through the case of Amy Johnson, the first woman to fly solo from England to Australia. Composed from old footage, radio reports, re-enactments and interviews, it was a less confrontational, astringent work, indicative of changing times and adapting strategies.

By the turn of the 1980s, the radical film movement in Britain had come to a historic pause, the landscape that had sustained it dramatically transformed by Thatcherism. Mulvey later wrote of the shock of this rupture, reflecting poignantly that in their preoccupation with questions of imagery and representation, their milieu had risked losing touch with more everyday commitments.[55] *Crystal Gazing* (1981), their fourth film together, was a product of this re-assessment. It marked a significant departure. A more conventionally dramatic film, occupied with the

---

[53] 'Together: Hitchcock and Len Lye', *Sight & Sound*, 1 July 1996, p. 34.
[54] 'Lee Russell Interviews Peter Wollen', p. 232.
[55] See Mulvey, introduction to first edition of *Visual and Other Pleasures*, p. xii.

contemporary social and political moment, it presented a portrait of the lives of four cultural workers in contemporary Notting Hill and Ladbroke Grove. Personal and intellectual crises are set against political strife and recession, which by its end intrude into the foreground. In its imagery and allusion, the film was engaged with the traditions of utopia, with the dialectics of hope and despair, optimism and pessimism. A melancholic work—they described it as an end of era movie—its outline was drawn from Erich Kästner's *Fabian. Die Geschichte eines Moralisten* (1932), written about the dying days of the Weimer Republic; Wollen once again drafted the screenplay.

As the funding for radical film dried up, a process of academicization occurred, with a broad move across both film and feminism into the universities. Culturally, a changing of the guard was underway, as a new generation of UK filmmakers emerged from the art schools with aesthetic sensibilities distinct from the comparative minimalism of low-budget counter-cinema. In the midst of this change, an initiative of the previous government, Channel 4, provided some temporary shelter. Founded with an emphasis on alternative broadcasting—Wollen had in fact lobbied to influence its remit in this direction with the Independent Filmmakers Association—it would be the venue for Wollen and Mulvey's final feature film.[56] *The Bad Sister* (1983) transmuted their conceptual interests into a high-theory made-for-TV movie, a psychoanalytic murder mystery oriented around the daughter's position in the Oedipus myth. Given a prime-time slot, it was watched by over two million people. Their projected next film was left unmade.

Recalibrations

In Wollen's writing, the beginning of the 1980s saw a moment of taking stock: 'Things look rather different nowadays. Modernism is in disarray and 68 has led to unanticipated disavowals and re-interpretations: the rollback has begun.'[57] A 1982 collection, *Readings and Writings: Semiotic Counter-Strategies*, brought together a range of work produced since 1968—his writings on the avant-gardes past and present, discussions of semiotics, a series of narrative analyses of Hollywood films employing Propp's morphologies, the narrative codes of Barthes and elements from Lacan and Freud, an essay re-casting *Citizen Kane* as a precursor

---

[56] See A. L. Rees, 'Experimenting on Air: UK artists' film on television', in *Experimental British Television*, Manchester 2007.
[57] 'The Avant-Gardes: Europe and America', *Framework*, Spring 1981, p. 9.

of modernism in the cinema rather than a monument of realism, meditations on film ontology and technology. It also included a set of short
stories—science-fiction inflected metafiction—an indication of the
wider cultural world that he moved in.[58] The preface described these
essays and fictions as 'part of the same heterogeneous corpus' as his
films with Mulvey, and stated that the division between theory and practice was one that a 'cultural counter-strategy' should seek to overcome.[59]
But while a repeated emphasis throughout falls on the import of this
work for developing a 'new cinema', the concluding essay, produced for
the volume, had a retrospective cast, retracing steps taken, and adopting
a tentative posture in the face of an uncertain future.[60]

Here, and in adjacent writings, Wollen described French theory—long
a source of inspiration—as now in a state of crisis. Recent tendencies,
exemplified by *Tel Quel* and to which *Screen* had not been immune,
had descended into irrationality, anti-scientism, the play of language
divorced from its referent, and were now being met by a revanchist
backlash, intent on sweeping away the legacy of 68. In this increasingly
hostile climate, Wollen stated that the project of semiotics was 'more
important to defend now than ever before', but within film, he submits,
its achievements had been circumscribed, failing to develop in a way
that could feed productively into film-making.[61] The project of developing a semiotics for the avant-garde had begun to seem 'more and more
Utopian'. This conclusion essentially marked the terminus of Wollen's
endeavours on this front. Some further discussions aside—an elegant
piece from 1984, 'Fire and Ice', exploring the grammar of photography
stands out—his thinking gravitated elsewhere.[62]

As for modernism, with a new arrangement between art and popular
culture now taking hold, Wollen insisted that the only route forward
for the ailing avant-garde film movement was a critical openness to the
popular arts, in keeping with the avant-garde's best traditions. Rather
than retreating to a mandarin ghetto, its examplars should be Brecht and

---

[58] These were published in *Bananas*, a literary magazine founded by the novelist
Emma Tennant in 1975.
[59] *Readings and Writings*, p. vii.
[60] 'Semiotic Counter-Strategies: Retrospect 1982', in *Readings and Writings*.
[61] 'The Avant-Gardes: Europe and America', p. 10.
[62] 'Fire and Ice', *Photographies*, March 1984. In the self-interview conducted with
'Lee Russell' of 1997, his alias probes him wryly on this subject: 'I don't mean to
sound sceptical, but what made you think that you could solve these problems with
yet another dose of linguistics?', p. 225.

Breton, revolutionary artists who strove to play a hegemonic role in the culture of their time. A sanguine prescription; signs of strain were more discernible elsewhere, as in a fractious dispute in the pages of *Screen*. The stimulus was an analysis of Manet's *Olympia* by T. J. Clark, which suggested that the painting's resistance to interpretation, rather than a radical and productive gesture, may instead have been a harmless play of signifiers, and in effect simply a failure of communication. Wollen replied vigorously, interpreting this as 'an attempt to undermine the whole paradigm of modernism and, specifically, the aesthetics of its radical avant-garde sector'. Such a position was in effect 'to turn one's back on the whole history of political art in this century'.[63] The strength of this response evinced his personal investment in the project of a radical aesthetics, now in retreat; the specific terms of Clark's argument—questions of audience and efficacy—carried a heightened charge at a moment of political restoration.

Perhaps the most striking feature of Wollen's reflections is that they chart a recalibration of his view of modern art. As the landscape had shifted, he argued, it had become clear that the break of cubism in fact provoked two competing tendencies: modernism, or the dominant strain of modernism, which pursued semiotic reduction, reflexivity, autonomy and detachment from the realm of reference, and the avant-garde, which was instead devoted to semiotic expansion, new relations between signifier and signified, heterogeneity and overcoming the extant boundaries of art.[64] The 'two avant-gardes' therefore required reassessment: instead of a field of difference within a unitary movement, he had been describing opposing forces. These had divergent histories: while the avant-garde was forced into retreat by political repression in 1930s Europe, in post-war America modernism had ascended to become the dominant expression of modernity. In recent decades, however, purity had steadily given way to heterogeneity, the doctrine of Greenberg ceding ground to the spirit of Duchamp. The burden of this was that the widely reported

---

[63] 'Manet: Modernism and Avant-Garde', *Screen*, Summer 1980, p. 25, responding to Clark's essay in the previous issue. Clark insisted that his intentions were more precise, that rather than a wholesale rejection he was arguing for an art with some form of representation and effective address. Notably he wrote that he was dissatisfied with his analysis and would reorient it when the final study was published. See *The Painting of Modern Life: Paris in the Art of Manet and his Followers*, Princeton 1985.

[64] Influential versions of this distinction have been set out by Peter Bürger in *Theory of the Avant-Garde*, Frankfurt 1974, and Andreas Huyssen in *After the Great Divide*, Bloomington 1986.

end of modernism, and the emergence of postmodernism, was not a sign that the avant-garde had run its course; rather it was a return of its many repressed instincts. Though modernism was coming to a close, the avant-garde would live on.

Radical curating

Ultimately, the new conjuncture saw a concerted shift in Wollen's activities, with an expansion of his remit to visual art as much as film, and to curation as well as writing. His major enterprises of the 1980s were exhibitions, critical explorations of the avant-garde and its history that probed the relation between radical art and revolutionary politics. 'When the future is unclear', he later explained of his turn to history, 'it's good to delve back into the past and see what looks new amid the old, what can be salvaged in an unexpected way, what gives a new twist to our perception of the present'.[65] The seeds of the first exhibition had been sown by a trip to Mexico in 1977 to visit Jon Halliday, then at El Colegio de México. The country had long been 'a kind of semi-mythical country, a site for the projection of dreams and fantasies' by artists and intellectuals; for Wollen himself, it became a key location in his critical imagination.[66] Above all, it was the Mexican Renaissance that captured his attention. As with the Russian avant-garde, it had been the progeny of revolution and civil war. Confronting similar issues—the relation of artist to public, competing demands of autonomy, functionalism, experimentalism, propaganda—it had navigated them differently, instead wedded to vernacular forms and to a re-enchantment of the pre-Columbian past.

The project that Wollen and Mulvey proposed to Mark Francis, then exhibition organizer at the Whitechapel Gallery, centred on two marginal figures from the movement, Frida Kahlo and Tina Modotti, both then largely unknown outside Mexico.[67] Wollen later reflected, with a certain regret, that the show's appearance in New York contributed to

[65] 'Lee Russell Interviews Peter Wollen', p. 247.

[66] 'Fridamania', NLR 22, July–August 2003, p. 128. Collected in *Paris Manhattan: Writings on Art*, London 2004.

[67] Whitechapel Gallery, London 1982, before travelling to Europe, America, and ending in Mexico City. Wollen and Mulvey also made an accompanying short documentary in 1983. Mark Francis would later move to the Centre Pompidou, then to the US, and Wollen would work with him on a number of further occasions: the Komar and Melamid show, the Situationist show, and the inaugural conference at the Warhol Museum, Pittsburgh, in 1995.

setting off 'Fridamania'.[68] For him in particular, their work represented a modern art that was expressly political, impure and open to popular culture. In retrospect, he wrote that he had been reaching towards a definition of postmodernism. Later in the decade, Wollen would scrutinize the movement's engagement with popular imagery more precisely, with an exhibition of José Guadalupe Posada, the printmaker and engraver whose work became emblematic for Rivera and his comrades of an authentic Mexican visual culture.[69]

Wollen also turned his attention to contemporary Russian art, curating an exhibition of the dissident artists Komar and Melamid in 1985.[70] This was an opportunity to reflect on what had emerged after the long winter of Stalinism, and to scan for any reanimation of the avant-garde. In its bricolage of styles, rejection of authenticity and purism, and openness to kitsch, the duo's work had a superficial similarity to the postmodernism now filling galleries in the West, but as Wollen emphasized, their work emerged from dramatically different coordinates. Rather than flattening out history, their project was a fundamentally historical one, working through the dislocation wrought by Stalinism's combination of ultra-Fordism and neo-tsarist counter-revolution. Likewise, the visual culture they drew from was that of socialist realism rather than consumer capitalism. Wollen likened their use of parody instead to the founding works of modern art, Manet's *Olympia* notably among them, with their charge of 'aggression and liberation', their appearance at thresholds between 'epochs and styles'.[71]

At the close of the decade, Wollen was one of the curators of a landmark exhibition of a post-war chapter of the avant-garde, the Situationist International.[72] The research prompted a magisterial essay

---

[68] See 'Fridamania', *Paris Manhattan*.

[69] 'Posada: Messenger of Mortality', 1989, travelled throughout Britain.

[70] Fruitmarket Gallery, Edinburgh, and the Museum of Modern Art, Oxford, their first major showing in Europe.

[71] 'Painting History', catalogue essay for the Komar and Melamid exhibition, pp. 39–40.

[72] 'On the passage of a few people through a rather brief moment in time. The Situationist International (1957–1972)', held at Centre Pompidou, February–April 1989; the exhibition later travelled to the ICA London, June–August 1989, and ICA Boston, October 1989–January 1990. Debord refused to be involved or attend. Not only was the exhibition held in a building named after the foe of 68, Pompidou, but it was the product of a redevelopment that had demolished a chunk of the Situationists' beloved Beaubourg.

reconstructing the movement's intellectual origins (through Breton and Lefebvre, Lukács and Sartre), the factions that fed into it, its developments, triumphs and schisms. By his account, the first phase of their activities was one of path-breaking artistic achievements. The union of art and politics however did not hold for long. A split soon emerged over whether art should be dissolved into a singular revolutionary praxis. This course condemned the movement to a fatal overpoliticization, leading to the effective elimination of art. In Wollen's portrait, the movement's dissolution marked both the end of an epoch in which avant-gardes had heroically aimed at the transfiguration of art, politics and everyday life, as well as the summation of Western Marxism. It was a conclusion with an obliquely autobiographical cast—May 68 'was both a curtain-call and a prologue, a turning-point in a drama we are all still blindly living'.'The Situationist International', Wollen concluded, 'left a legacy of great value. The wasteful luxury of utopian projects, however doomed, is no bad thing. We need not persist in seeking a unique condition for revolution, but neither need we forget the desire for liberation. We move from place to place and from time to time. This is true of art as well as politics.'[73]

An anniversary essay for *Film Comment*, '68/88: Thinking Theory', dealt more specifically with the study of film since the writing of *Signs and Meaning*. Auteurism had been victorious and was now 'part of the general wisdom', semiotics had provided the 'necessary explosion' for dramatic advances in film theory, while the wider push for cinema to be recognized as a field of study had proved successful. An inevitable diminishment of energies had accompanied the institutionalization of the discipline, though a 'rebel impulse' was retained in some quarters. The assessment however concluded in a melancholy key: academicization threatened to cut film theory off from film practice, and though Wollen had come to reconsider his belief that the two could be simply united, traffic between them remained essential. More significantly, a 'depressing irony of history' may be that at the same time as its move into the academy, film is passing into history: 'To be brutal about it, film is about to become an art form of the past as we enter deep into the electronic age.' Confronting these new technologies would require thinking through these new systems of 'signs and meaning', and recapturing the 'determination and willingness to defy common sense and set out on a new theoretical project'.[74]

---

[73] 'The Situationist International', NLR 1/174, March–April 1989, pp. 72, 95.
[74] '68/88: Thinking Theory', p. 51.

With the avant-garde film scene passed, cinema as a whole now seemed to be reaching an end. Wollen did however direct a film of his own in these years, his only solo feature as a director, the remarkable *Friendship's Death* (1987). He had been in Amman in 1970, as a journalist on assignment for *Seven Days*, during 'Black September', the Jordanian Army's attack on the PLO-controlled territories. This 'somewhat hair-raising experience' was transmuted into science-fiction, the conflict refracted through the perception of a crash-landed extra-terrestrial—Tilda Swinton, in one of her first screen roles.[75] Shot in a fortnight, on a set consisting of two hotel rooms, Wollen proudly described it as a B-movie, associating it with other politically charged low budget films being made in Britain. A poignant, discursive film, stylistically it was poles apart from his work with Mulvey. Wollen described it as dealing with the questions of aesthetics and politics that had long concerned him, only adapted to a different cultural climate, in which the terms of debate, context, financing and audiences had all changed.

Metropolis of the spectacle

Throughout the decade, Wollen had continued to make ends meet with temporary teaching roles, upping sticks for a semester or more in New York or Rhode Island, San Francisco or Vancouver. In 1988, this took him to Los Angeles to teach film at UCLA.[76] After a few years of temporary contracts, and a stint at Vassar, he was given a permanent position—suddenly at fifty, gaining steady employment and enrolled on a pension plan. He settled there with the writer Leslie Dick, whom he met in 1984; they would have a daughter, Audrey, in 1992, and marry in 1993. The 'Capital of the Spectacle', as Wollen signed his exposition of the Situationist International, would show up in various of his endeavours— its geography, architecture and car culture, its racism and police violence. Of Hitchcock's parallel change of residency, Wollen suggested that he 'needed Los Angeles but, in the depths of his dreams and nightmares, he never left London'.[77] Wollen also lived a somewhat divided life; what

---

[75] 'Airports: A Personal Memoir', *Here There Elsewhere*, London 2002, p. 94. See 'Two Weeks on Another Planet: An Interview with Peter Wollen', *Monthly Film Bulletin*, November 1987. Posthumously, *Friendship's Death* was selected for screening at Cannes Classics 2020; the BFI's belated 4K remastering of the film will be released on Blu-ray/DVD on 7 December 2020.

[76] Wollen was a devoted teacher, admired by his students. For one personal account of his influence, see Victoria Duckett, 'The lecturer's legacy: In memory of Professor Peter Wollen', *Senses of Cinema*, January 2020.

[77] 'Hitch: A Tale of Two Cities (London and Los Angeles)', *Paris Hollywood*, p. 73.

he gained in stability, he lost in community. Nevertheless, the three of them would return to London for the summer months, and enjoyed a sabbatical year in 1997–98, giving parties and seeing friends in their flat overlooking Westbourne Grove.

The change of circumstances proved auspicious for his work. The 1990s were richly productive years, in which Wollen produced dozens of articles, papers and essays, and worked on a range of exhibitions, catalogues and collections that reached across the visual culture of the modern. Far from sequestered by a move into the academy, Wollen travelled often, with conferences, symposia, exhibitions and film festivals taking him to Buffalo or Salt Lake City, Maastricht or São Paulo, Moscow or Cairo. It was not in his nature to turn down an invitation or a plane ticket. His preferred way of working was to a brief, for a request or occasion; once the structure of the argument was clear in his mind, he wrote quickly, with minimal editing or reconfiguring. His activities also in some respects turned outwards. Amongst the projects of his early years at UCLA were a set of arts documentaries made with Tariq Ali for Channel 4.[78] He became a regular writer of arts journalism, from 1991 a contributor to his old bête noire *Sight & Sound*, from 1994 to the *London Review of Books*, where many of his finest writings on the visual arts and its neighbouring territories appeared.[79]

Having been a partisan for semiotics and theory, the primary mode of this multifarious work, whether for academia, journalism or the art world, was in fact historiography, closer to the treatment of Eisenstein that opened *Signs and Meaning* than the prescriptions of its later chapters.[80] While earlier writing had been polemically driven, his engagements now tended to be more exploratory, delving into the everyday life of cultural

---

[78] Two distinctive films of ideas and politics, the first on Komar and Melamid, the second on the photographer Milton Rogovin.

[79] Penelope Houston had retired from *Sight & Sound* in 1990, after almost 35 years as editor.

[80] Psychoanalysis endured as a metalanguage, particularly for his writings on film— *Vertigo* is 'a visual encyclopaedia of psychopathology', Eisenstein's development as a director was hindered by his repressed sexuality, Hawks's films are depictions of philobatism and ocnophilia, and so on ('Compulsion', *Sight & Sound*, April 1997, pp. 14–16; 'Introduction', *Howard Hawks: American Artist*, p. 6; 'Perhaps', *October*, Spring 1999). In 'An Alphabet of Cinema' he describes cinephilia as the 'symptom of a desire to remain within the child's view of the world', always fascinated by a 'mysterious parental drama' and seeking to 'master one's anxiety by compulsive repetition', p. 119.

history, following lines of influence and development, often taking unexpected turns, detours, deviations. Hollywood also once more became a field of enquiry. One early project was an auteurist study of *Singin' in the Rain* (1992), which celebrated Gene Kelly's genius for merging popular cinema with popular dance, as Chaplin had done with mime, and lamented the derailment of his career by McCarthyism. In a further sign of changing times, this was produced for the BFI—Wollen dedicated it to the memory of Paddy Whannel. He subsequently co-edited an anthology of Hawks criticism for them.

Notably, there was in large part a closure of his personal canon; he remained wedded to the classic period heralded by *Cahiers*. His contributions to *Sight & Sound*, for instance, on occasion dealt with a new release, but these were used as opportunities for exploring wider subjects.[81] His pieces on Welles or Ray or Hawks were, by contrast, richly engaged with the intellectual, artistic and production history of their films. Hollywood directors of later generations—Scorsese, Altman, Lynch, Tarantino—received no equivalent treatment. Hitchcock, meanwhile, remained for him 'the most compelling and current of filmmakers', and continued to prompt his investigation.[82] While 'ruthlessness' had been an early maxim, Wollen's auteurism was now stimulated by affection. It was a testament to his independence of spirit that a newfound proximity to Hollywood did nothing to alter this orientation.

Distance, by contrast, seemed to prompt an engagement with British film. A common property here was countering the received idea of it as indelibly realist. Treatments of the cycle of 'Spiv' films, a transmutation of *film noir* that thrived in the 1940s, as also of Carol Reed and Michael Powell, Nicholas Roeg and Terry Gilliam, Derek Jarman and Peter Greenaway, emphasized a lineage of romanticism, melodrama and fantasy. Another interest was Britain's relation to modernism. An appreciation, written in 1993, of the generation of British filmmakers that had followed his own—those formed by the cultural excitements of the sixties (pop, the counter-culture, post-68 avant-garde film) and radicalized by Thatcherism—suggested that they represented the 'Last

[81] The only essay in *Paris Hollywood: Writings on Film* about a recent Hollywood film proves the rule: 'Blade Runner', pp. 123–33, originally published in 1998, is a discussion of Los Angeles and the rise of the world city, in dialogue with Mike Davis's *City of Quartz*.
[82] 'The Players: A Film Comment Poll', *Film Comment*, Jan–Feb 2000, p. 61. This was in response to a question about the best film figure of the 1990s.

New Wave', and a belated flourishing of modernism in Britain.[83] The geography of modernism, Wollen argued, related to levels of development; the wrench of modernity registering violently elsewhere but weakly in the homeland of the Industrial Revolution. A spate of intricate essays, written for the LRB in the mid-90s, dealing with the artistic culture of the first decades of the century (featuring Beardsley, Bloomsbury and Woolf, Rupert Brooke and others), elucidated the ways in which it took only temporary hold. Modernism, in Wollen's portrayal, was fed by a turbulent culture of alternative views and lifestyles, which for reasons of class, politics or sensibility, repelled the leaders of English arts and letters. Its few committed practitioners were expatriates finding a temporary bolthole; energies from abroad were integrated and diffused, only finally blossoming in the upheavals of the sixties.

Recasting modernism

This analysis of Britain's attenuated experience of modernism was a subsidiary of the major product of Wollen's first years in California. *Raiding the Icebox: Reflections on Twentieth-Century Culture* (1993)—a book with strong claims to be his magnum opus—brought together seven substantial essays published in some form between 1987 and 1990, which span the history of modernism from its emergence to its dissolution. These present a series of interconnected episodes: the orientalist vogue spearheaded by Diaghilev, Poiret and Matisse; the rise of 'Americanism' with its fetishism of machine and production line; Pollock, Greenberg and the triumph of American painting; Warhol and Pop; two episodes, the Situationist International and Komar and Melamid, from his earlier exhibitions; and finally the rise of para-tourist art in a new era of cultural exchange. The mutations of arts and ideas are set, most prominently, in the context of the rise, development and eventual transformation of Fordism. The book's title, drawn from Warhol, sits at its mid-point, where mass consumption and the domestication of modern technology finally registered in the sphere of high culture, at a moment when the epoch of the golden age began to show its first signs of crisis.

Together, the chapters provide a vivid panorama of the art of the century that is matched by few other accounts. The lack of an introduction or preface—the reflex of an avant-gardist's sensibility perhaps—which might have set out its intentions or suggested how the pieces fitted

---

[83] 'The Last New Wave', *Paris Hollywood*.

together, surely lessened its impact. In the book's final pages, Wollen writes that it had been originally conceived as an inquiry into post-modernism, but that he had come to believe this impossible without a fresh inquiry into the concept of modernism. This is the kernel of his most persistently stressed argument, one that had been first formu-lated a decade earlier: that postmodernism can be best understood as the re-emergence of long-suppressed elements. In this sense, the book develops, on a grand scale, his vision of a century animated by compet-ing aesthetic visions and practices. 'Modernism' here is employed as an overarching category, comprised of various strands, dominant and latent; the avant-garde portrayed as a pioneering element within it, pressing for heterogeneity against purism, for dismantling barriers rather than forti-fying them. In his narrative, at its birth modern art entailed a circulation between high and low, core and periphery, and its challenge to the *ancien régime* of taste was with an aesthetic of 'difference, excess, hybridity and polysemy', but this was subsumed by a machine-oriented functional-ism during modernism's consolidation.[84] An equivalent dynamic then played out in the post-war, with the supremacy of modernist painting defined in opposition to mass culture, until a storming of the galleries by kitsch re-established contact with the vernacular.

With this revolt against purist orthodoxy, Wollen's account turned from the art of the West to that of the post-colonial world. While at its incep-tion, modernism had drawn resources from the periphery (the Mexican Renaissance a rare exception), Wollen portrayed this circulation as now set into reverse. The unprecedented expansion of global tourism was stimulating the art of the post-colonial world into new areas of origi-nality and complexity. He concludes with a vision of sterility in the metropolis, and imaginative renewal in the periphery. 'Modernism', he writes, in one of the book's many arresting passages, 'is being succeeded not by a totalizing Western postmodernism but by a hybrid new aes-thetic in which the new corporate forms of communication and display will be constantly confronted by new vernacular forms of invention and expression. Creativity always comes from beneath, it always finds an unexpected and indirect path forward and it always makes use of what it can scavenge by night.'[85]

In this last majestic movement, with its emphasis on a burgeoning periphery and the perennial emergence of art from below, the political

---

[84] *Raiding the Icebox: Reflections on Twentieth-Century Culture*, London, 1993, p. 206.
[85] *Raiding the Icebox*, pp. 209–10.

and economic forces that undergird the account as a whole are less present. In the same year that *Raiding the Icebox* was published, however, Wollen produced an essay reckoning with the political dispensation of the postmodern, in the form of an appraisal of Kautsky. In it, he described having recently read *Bolshevism at a Deadlock* (1931) for the first time with astonishment, finding a book 'written with such trenchancy and foresight, six decades before the events that it predicts'.[86] Wollen accounts for the belatedness of this discovery by Kautsky's marginalization: a major figure of Marxism at the time, he was an early and outspoken critic of the path taken by the Bolsheviks and became an isolated figure as the workers' movement polarized, whose emphases also denied him a resurgence in the climate of 68. Insisting that now was an opportune moment for rediscovery of Kautsky's writings on representative democracy, the conditions for socialism and ultra-imperialism, Wollen concluded that with the end of the Cold War, it was time for 'a redefinition, even a re-foundation, of socialism in the West', one in which socialists accepted a realistic hope, 'however historically distant', rather than a false one.

This statement was unusual in its directness; politics in these years was mostly a substrate of Wollen's writing. Rarely absent, when it surfaced it often did so with considerable force. A catalogue essay of 1997, written to accompany an exhibition of post-60s Californian art, had occasion to lament a structure of feeling in which history appeared to have no direction, art no redemptive task: in such circumstances, 'we mourn for a meaningless future'.[87] A second clash with T. J. Clark was also testimony to resolute political sentiment. Along with another former member of the Situationist International, Clark produced an essay damning recent assessments of the movement, including Wollen's.[88] Replying gracefully, he was nevertheless hurt by the personal animus of the criticism, which cast him—astoundingly—as an enemy of 68. That upsurge continued to hold great resonance for him: '1968', he wrote that same year, 'was an emblematic moment which spectacularized the idea of change itself,

---

[86] 'Our Post-Communism: The Legacy of Karl Kautsky', NLR 1/202, Nov–Dec 1993, pp. 90, 93.
[87] 'Vectors of Melancholy' in *Scene of the Crime*, 1997, p. 34. Exhibition at Hammer Museum, Los Angeles, curated by Ralph Rugoff. Wollen anticipates 'leaving a century of war, crash, depression, segregation, holocaust, nuclear annihilation, world domination, assassination, body bags, junk bonds, underclass', p. 33.
[88] A piece by Régis Debray was the immediate target. This took place in the pages of *October*. See 'Why Art Can't Kill the Situationist International', *October* 79, Winter 1997. Wollen's response was carried in the following number.

but, as always, history plays strange tricks and the change which came wasn't the one that had been expected. It was the end of Fordism, the end of Keynesianism, the end of classic social democracy, the beginning of a new world order, constructed around a string of world cities linked by a lattice of electronic communications which facilitated a sweeping reconfiguration of world capital'.[89] In such moments, the imagery with which Wollen described historical change—strange tricks, unexpected reversals, close cousins of the knight's move—appears as a form of consolation for the fortunes of the radicalism to which he had staked his allegiance, one that held onto the promise of its re-emergence.

The lineaments of *Raiding the Icebox*—the challenge to orthodox readings of modernism, the global turn, the persistent lineage of the avant-garde; these, along with some lesser motifs, were pursued throughout the rest of the decade. Warhol, central protagonist of the revolt against purism, prompted two further essays, which set his career in the context of parallel upheavals in the world of art and fashion.[90] Fashion's role in modern art, introduced by his account of Poiret, became a consistent subject of inquiry, whose most sustained expression was 'Addressing the Century', an exhibition of their modern relationship held in London in 1998. It was a history with recognizable stresses: the boundaries of the realm of art, the circulation of high and low, convergences and divergences, the emancipation from conservative strictures.[91] An adjacent essay treated this last development more critically: while the current era presented opportunities for unprecedented dialogue and interplay, it was in the context of their joint incorporation into a global society of the spectacle, in which any new artistic possibilities were outweighed by wider perils.[92] The role of dance in the century's art was similarly addressed in a number of pieces: an essay on Weimar Germany, published in 1995, for instance, followed its treacherous path from Cabaret

---

[89] 'Lee Russell Interviews Peter Wollen', pp. 246–7.

[90] See 'Plastics—The Magical and the Prosaic' in *The Warhol Look: Glamour, Style, Fashion*, New York 1997, and 'Andy Warhol: Renaissance Man' in *Who is Andy Warhol?*, London 1997.

[91] 'Addressing the Century: 100 Years of Art & Fashion', co-curated with Fiona Bradley, Hayward Gallery in London, 1998–99. Wollen's final piece dealing with fashion concerned *The Arcades Project*: it described how Benjamin was enraptured by the protean nature of fashion, seeing it both as 'an object lesson in commodity culture and a possibility of messianic redemption'. Wollen speculates this would have been the work's conclusion if Benjamin had been able to complete it. 'The Concept of Fashion in *The Arcades Project*', *boundary 2*, Spring 2003, p. 142.

[92] 'Art and Fashion: Friends or Enemies?', *Paris Manhattan*, pp. 180–1.

Voltaire to the Berlin Olympiad. Though in a different register, such endeavours shared something of their impetus with Wollen's first critical project, which had pitched itself against the exclusion of a popular medium from the humanities, and its subordinate position in the hierarchy of the arts.[93]

The global came to animate his work in a variety of forms—through explorations of cosmopolitanism, both its history and continued promise; the cultural ramifications of the world city; the pressure imposed on the cultures of the periphery by the new era of globalization; indications, however imperfect or incipient, of egalitarian exchange and growing global intermingling. Most prominently, it was the inflection given to a further chapter in his history of modern art, the exhibition he co-curated in 1999, 'Global Conceptualism'.[94] 'Conceptual art', he argued in an accompanying essay on the movement's origins and effects, 'just as it de-centred the traditional aesthetics and semantics of visual representation—also de-centred New York itself from its hegemonic position in the global art world'.[95] In his rendering, this was the first fully international avant-garde, whose effect was not only to seal the fate of modernism, but to dethrone painting and sculpture—'the single greatest shift in art since the Renaissance'—for a field of unprecedented heterogeneity. Unleashing tendencies which continued to develop globally, Wollen suggests that these had 'proved resistant to those powerful forces of homogeneity and domination which come inevitably with economic and cultural globalization'.

With the historic shift of energy from the metropolis at the close of modernism, Wollen's treatment of the contemporary art of the West became more infrequent, his critical attention drawn back to earlier ruptures far more than to what emerged in their wake. Symptomatically, an exhibition of the collection of Charles Saatchi, patron of the YBAs, which he reviewed for the LRB in 1997, provoked his scepticism. Hirst, Emin et al were 'Thatcher's Artists', whatever their disdain for conservative social values; their breakout show had been the art-world equivalent of the City of London's Big Bang, inaugurating British art's entry into the new

93 'Tales of Total Art and Dreams of the Total Museum' in Lynne Cooke and Peter Wollen, eds, *Visual Display: Culture Beyond Appearances*, Seattle 1995.
94 The exhibition was 'Global Conceptualism: Points of Origin, 1950s–1980s', Queens Museum, New York 1999.
95 See Wollen's catalogue essay, 'Global Conceptualism and North American Art', in *Paris Manhattan*, pp. 32, 28, 34.

global economy.[96] Beyond the proliferation of familiar installation art, Wollen however found unexpected innovation in the painting on show, its demotion seeming to have prompted some reassessment of the modernist legacy, at odds with the dominant impulse of art as stepping stone to 'the seductive new world of celebrity, commercialism and sensation'. Continued signs of life were found in a number of places. Alongside intellectual portraits of earlier figures, Wollen produced some of more recent artists that caught his interest, finding much to appreciate in the work of Tacita Dean, Julie Becker and Liam Gillick.[97]

From Z to A

At the turn of the millennium, Wollen was working at full tilt. Amongst his endeavours of that year were essays about Magritte's bowler hat, Huston's biopic of Freud, Jarman's final film, the role of kitsch in art, the cultural history of the military tank, the philosophy of time in the cinema, the political role of ballet in the reign of Louis XIV (a rare venture back to earlier centuries), and an edited collection on the culture of the car. By 2002 however, he had begun to show signs of what would later be diagnosed as early-onset Alzheimer's, a hereditary condition that had afflicted his mother. An appalling fate for a mind that moved so quickly and so freely, Wollen refused to submit, working until he was no longer able. These were terrible years for him and his family, leading only towards tragedy. Two collections, *Paris Hollywood: Writings on Film* (2002) and *Paris Manhattan: Writings on Art* (2004), brought together some of the work from his last decade. In December 2005, he was admitted into a care home. His final essay for the LRB was a return to the Russian avant-garde, specifically Malevich, for him the most provocative and enigmatic of its painters. It concluded with the same vignette of Malevich's funeral that had closed 'Art in Revolution' three decades earlier, once again with a prophecy of resurrection. Malevich's goal had been to create art representing 'his own vision of the future, rather than the everyday reality that dismayed him', and despite the adversity faced by the avant-garde, he held firmly to the belief that it would prevail.

What can be said to characterize Wollen's final batch of writings? The essay on Malevich was one of many which returned to subjects

---

[96] 'Thatcher's Artists', LRB, 30 October 1997.
[97] 'Tacita Dean', *Afterall* 1, 1999, pp. 105–115; 'Julie Becker', *Afterall* 2, 2000, pp. 20–26; 'Liam Gillick: Thought Experiments', *Parkett* 61, 2001, pp. 76–82.

of enduring interest—the Russian avant-garde, Eisenstein, Hawks, Hitchcock, Renoir, Godard, the *nouvelle vague*—to offer last assessments, often with reformulations. What he had previously conceived as Eisenstein's retreat to symbolism could in fact be better understood as a confrontation with the arrival of sound and colour, one which marked an advance towards 'his great dream of aesthetic totality'.[98] Rather than fragments shored up against ruin, Godard's aesthetics of quotation instead bears glimmers of essential humanist values. An essay about the pioneering ethnographic filmmaker Jean Rouch, meanwhile, reflected that his own conception of 'counter-cinema' had drawn a great deal from what Godard had in turn learnt from Rouch—from his erasure of 'the false line between documentary and drama, between camera as recording instrument and camera as catalyst for performance'.[99] Others turned to figures little discussed in his critical work but which, like Burroughs— an early inspiration and acquaintance in the sixties—or Kathy Acker—a lover in the early eighties—had a biographical resonance. A beautiful piece about Antonioni begins with Wollen's first encounter with his work in the early sixties, revealing that he no longer saw the films through the critical paradigms of the period, but as revolving around 'a personal and very private way of looking at the world'.[100] Tight-lipped about his own contribution to Antonioni's oeuvre, he concludes with a consideration of *The Passenger's* bravura penultimate shot: 'Like all of Antonioni's work, it makes a demand on our patience. Patience, Antonioni once wrote, is "also a trait of love": this loving patience, this waiting, observing, are the vital signs of Antonioni's cinema.'

This was one of many final pieces that carried a personal inflection. A meditation on avant-garde film—describing how it 'must always veer away from the beaten path into the shifting sands of the unclassified and unsettled, embracing the polymorphously perverse, hovering between narration and abstraction, concept and drama'—apologises for being 'shamelessly autobiographical' in places.[101] Others shimmer with stray intimate details, by turns comic or profound. Though little inclined to sustained autobiographical writing, Wollen produced a few oblique and playful exercises in this vein during his last writing years. 'Airports: A Personal Memoir' lists every airport he could remember visiting and the

---

[98] 'Perhaps', *October* 88, Spring 1999, p. 50.
[99] 'Jean Rouch', *Paris Hollywood*, p. 101.
[100] 'Caro Antonioni', *Afterall* 3, 2001, pp. 35, 38.
[101] 'Knight's Moves', pp. 160, 147.

memories they conjured, creating a record of an itinerant life of art and film led by an eclectic curiosity. 'An Alphabet of Cinema', composed in tribute to the *Cahiers* editor Serge Daney, presents a wilfully idiosyncratic A–Z, beginning with A for Aristotle—Wollen makes a case for him as the first film theorist—that brims with reflections and anecdotes from Wollen's cinephilia and involvement with film. These, and other final writings, had a distinctly experimental quality, with the essay as the end product of a set of rules or an imaginative procedure. An artful last engagement with the Situationists, addressing their approach to architecture, for instance, did so in a manner Wollen described as a '*dérive* from minaret to outsider garden'.[102] The *dérive*, like the knight's move, might be seen as a wider principle for Wollen, present in some capacity in much of his writing, but most pronounced in these later strolls through the art and film of the century.

What of valedictory statements? Reaching Z in his 'Alphabet of Cinema'— it stands for *Zorn's Lemma, Zero for Conduct* and Godard's maxim: 'back to zero'—he signed off with a call to arms. Having previously forecast that the artform of the twentieth century was headed for extinction, here Wollen revealed a change of perspective. 'As we enter the age of new media, the cinema is re-inventing itself. We need to see that re-invention in radical as well as mainstream terms, to try and re-imagine the cinema as it might have been and as, potentially, it still could be—an experimental art, constantly renewing itself, as a counter-cinema, as'—and here he was quoting Daney—'"cinema haunted by writing". Back to zero. Begin again. A is for Avant-Garde.'[103]

---

[102] 'The Situationists and Architecture', *Paris Manhattan*, p. 218.
[103] The original quote comes from 'Les Cahiers du cinéma 1968–1977: Interview with Serge Daney', *The Thousand Eyes*, no. 2, 1977.

independent thinking from polity

Not One Less
Mourning, Disobedience and Desire
María Pia López

López, a founding member and active participant in the Not One Less protest, offers a first-hand account of the distinctive characteristics and lineages of this popular feminist movement, while examining the broader issues of gender politics and violence, inequality and social justice, mourning, performance and protest that are relevant to all contemporary societies.

CRITICAL SOUTH SERIES
PB 978-1-5095-3192-9 | £15.99 | July 2020

Cryptocommunism
Mark Alizart

"*A fascinating antidote to reductive takes on cryptocurrencies. Blockchains are more than just cryptolibertarianism and this book makes a provocative and wide-ranging case for just how important they might be.*"
Nick Srnicek, King's College London

PB 978-1-5095-3858-4 | £9.99 | July 2020

Is Free Speech Racist?
Gavan Titley

Where there is intense political contestation and public confusion as to what constitutes racism and who gets to define it, 'free speech' has been adopted as a primary mechanism for amplifying and re-animating racist ideas and racializing claims. As such, contemporary free speech discourse reveals much about the ongoing life of race and racism in contemporary society.

DEBATING RACE SERIES
PB 978-1-5095-3616-0 | £9.99 | July 2020

Kracauer
A Biography
Jörg Später

"*Später avoids simple description and banal interpretations and surprises the reader with careful, considered judgements, thus demonstrating what a biographer should fundamentally be: a courageous historian.*"
Thomas Meyer, Süddeutsche Zeitung

HB 978-1-5095-3301-5 | £35.00 | July 2020

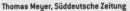

Go to **www.politybooks.com** to order   @politybooks   facebook.com/politybooks

⊂P COUNTERPRESS

ART, LAW, POWER: PERSPECTIVES ON LEGALITY AND RESISTANCE IN CONTEMPORARY AESTHETICS

Editors: Lucy Finchett-Maddock & Eleftheria Lekakis

"Exploring how the affective qualities of the arts interplay with the effective capacities of the law, this collection offers a new, and vitally important, perspective on the field."

— Stephen Duncombe, Co-Director of the Center for Artistic Activism and Professor of Media and Culture, New York University

ETHICS OF TRAGEDY: DWELLING, THINKING, MEASURING

Ari Hirvonen

"This is a hugely important intervention into our thinking about tragedy and how such thinking holds up a black mirror for our times. Ari Hirvonen is the Jari Litmanen of philosophy. Highly recommended."

— Simon Critchley, Hans Jonas Professor of Philosophy, New School for Social Research

DECOLONIZING SEXUALITIES: TRANSNATIONAL PERSPECTIVES, CRITICAL INTERVENTIONS

Editors: Sandeep Bakshi, Suhraiya Jivraj, & Silvia Posocco

"The volume is more than timely ... it is centred on narratives of solidarity and alliance which are so important today in a world under the assault of financial capitalism, new politics of dispossession and colonization, and new politics of division and fragmentation."

— Françoise Verges (Chair Global South(s), College d'études mondiales, Paris)

https://counterpress.org.uk

READ ABOUT OUR "FAIR ACCESS" POLICY

LOLA SEATON

PAINTING

NATIONALISM GREEN?

I N THE SURREAL dénouement of a recent episode of the *New York Times* podcast 'The Daily', Doug Hurley, one of three US astronauts currently orbiting 250 miles above the Earth aboard the International Space Station, suggested that civilian space travel might prove a balm for global ills like 'the pandemic and the strife in the cities' following the police killing of George Floyd:

> When you look out the window, when you see the planet below, you don't see borders. You don't see the strife. You see this beautiful planet that we need to take care of. And hopefully, as technology advances and as this commercial space travel gets going, more people will get that opportunity. Because I think if you get the chance to look out the window from space and look back on our planet . . . you'll realize that this is one big world, rather than all these different little countries or cities or factions that we have on the planet. And I think it will make it a better place.[1]

If this startling plug for the utopian promise of space tourism—its commodified experience of sublimity prompting epiphanies about the artifice of territorial divisions and activating a latent eco-consciousness, thus saving the planet one cosmic sightseer at a time—represents an extreme version of one kind of environmentalism, which envisions the transcendence of national boundaries through an enlightened recognition of our collective embeddedness in the ecosphere, Anatol Lieven takes the diametrically opposite view. His latest book *Climate Change and the Nation State* argues that the self-interest of nation-states should not be suppressed in pursuit of global solutions to anthropogenic climate change, but doubled down on.[2]

That nation-states, rather than intergovernmental bodies or some emergent supranational sovereign, will—if anyone will—be the vanguard of
response to the climate crisis is not the central claim of Lieven's book;
their ongoing centrality as political units and global actors is assumed
rather than lengthily argued for. The question animating Lieven's
contribution to green strategizing is rather about what will compel
nation-states to act, and what will motivate their increasingly polarized
electorates to rally behind some version of a Green New Deal (GND), of
which Lieven is firmly in favour.[3] The way Lieven formulates his version
of this cardinal climate question—what is to be done?—is conditioned
by his diagnosis of the current impasse. Nation-states' negligence hith-
erto, Lieven argues, proceeds not from a lack of capacity, financial or
technological—an uncontroversial claim, given the immense resources
mustered by governments in response to the pandemic—but 'the lack of
mobilization of elites all over the world, and of voters in the West'.

Climate Change and the Nation State is thus an appeal to 'sensible and
patriotic policymakers' everywhere but is 'mainly directed at audiences
in the Western democracies'—and the US in particular, which is pre-
dictably the nation-state with which Lieven is primarily concerned. This
bias is in some ways justified—aside from its hegemonic status and out-
sized influence on global affairs, the US emits more carbon per capita
than any other country in the world—but also seems a contingent effect
of timing: the book is palpably inflected by the looming US presidential election. In Lieven's view, one of the reasons climate change has
remained lethally low on the official political agenda in the US and elsewhere is that environmentalism has become excessively associated with
'cultural liberalism', alienating the conservative voters who most need to
be won to the planetary cause.[4] Particularly in the US, the climate crisis

---

[1] 'Counting the Infected', The Daily podcast, *New York Times*, 8 July 2020.
[2] Anatol Lieven, *Climate Change and the Nation State: The Realist Case*, London
2020. Hereafter CCNS.
[3] 'One version or another of a Green New Deal is the only way to go', CCNS, p. 92.
[4] Lieven's mapping of this liberal-conservative opposition onto the Democratic and
Republican parties is at best anachronistic. Lieven presents 'cultural liberalism'—a
rubric he never defines, but under which he groups such 'ideological luxuries' as
'open borders, free migration', 'identity politics', 'the Woke movement', 'the Me
Too movement'—as spanning seemingly any political affiliation to the left of the
GOP. He refers to Democrats, liberals, 'the left', or even 'the Greens' (glossing over
right-wing environmentalists) interchangeably—collapsing these political distinctions on the apparent assumption that, whatever their differences on the economy,
for example, they converge on social or cultural issues, as well as on the climate
crisis: CCNS, p. xxv.

has become an identitarian issue, which precludes its emergence as a bipartisan one. According to the Pew Research Center, in the US 'partisanship is a stronger factor in people's beliefs about climate change than is their level of knowledge and understanding about science'; a 2018 Pew survey found that 83 per cent of Democrats regard climate change as a major threat compared to only 27 per cent of Republicans—a 56-point difference.[5] As Lieven puts it, disbelief in or disregard for the devastating consequences of burning fossil fuels has become a matter of conservative 'communal culture; like owning guns or attending church'. The climate-sceptic right says 'Not "We are not *convinced* by the evidence of climate change" but "We aren't *the kind of people* who believe in climate change"'. This partisanship is a major impediment to the creation of 'a new national dispensation in national politics akin to the original New Deal', which Lieven believes will be necessary to deliver green parties 'sweeping majorities' in 'repeated elections'.[6]

What, then, does Lieven propose to overcome the liberal ideological monopoly on ecological concern? His first concrete proposal for transforming the climate crisis into a solid national priority in the US and other Western democracies is to discursively reframe global warming as an imminent threat to national security: 'the US military needs to throw its full weight behind the Green New Deal'. 'Securitizing' global warming would at once depoliticize the issue—'remove it from the natural sphere of politics'—and render it more consonant with conservative political cultures, since enlisting military figures in the rhetorical detoxification of the topic would, Lieven hopes, have particular influence with Republicans, military functionaries being among the few experts who command respect across the political spectrum.[7]

Lieven worked for the FT and *The Times* in the mid-80s and 90s, covering first Afghanistan and Pakistan—the subject of his *Pakistan: A Hard Country* (2011)—and then the former Soviet Union. In the early 2000s, he began writing about international relations and security for US research centres; since 2006, he has taught at Georgetown's Qatar

---

[5] A similar pattern exists in Europe, though to a lesser degree, with supporters of the AfD, UKIP and Rassemblement National respectively 28, 22 and 21 per cent less likely to view climate change as a major threat than non-supporters. See the Pew Research Center: Cary Funk and Brian Kennedy, 'How Americans See Climate Change and the Environment in 7 Charts', 21 April 2020; and Moira Fagan and Christine Huang, 'A Look at How People Around the World View Climate Change', 18 April 2019.

[6] CCNS, pp. 132, 10, xiv.   [7] CCNS, p. 7.

campus.[8] Lieven's 'securitization' idea has its origins in a minor professional crisis, narrated in the introduction, which confers on the ensuing book a winning atmosphere of sincerity. Reflecting on the full meaning of the climate crisis prompted him to realize 'the comparative irrelevance of most of the issues on which I have been working in the areas of international relations and security studies'. Researching the escalating tensions between the US and China over the atolls of the South China Sea, the thought dawned on him that in the long term 'these places will be meaningless for both sides', since 'rising sea-levels and intensified typhoons will have put the sources of these tensions under water again'. Noting the absurdity of such territorial spats and geopolitical rivalries, as well as their 'destructive effects' on 'international co-operation against climate change', not to mention the environmental havoc wrought by militarization more generally, Lieven appeals to political elites to realize that 'the long-term interests of the world's great powers are far more threatened by climate change than they are by each other'. This sounds straightforward—a policy shift prompted by a sober consideration of the terrifying consequences of unchecked carbon emissions—but it would involve a radical reboot of national priorities. For one of the primary techniques for protecting national security as it is currently conceived is pursuing energy self-sufficiency or 'resource independence' by using increasingly invasive technologies to unearth domestic fossil-fuel reserves.

Asymmetrical impacts

In what sense does climate change immediately threaten the national security of Western states? Unlike India, Pakistan and Bangladesh, for example—first, second and fourth on HSBC's 2018 report ranking countries' vulnerability to climate change—and notwithstanding Californian wildfires and the vulnerability of Eastern coastal cities to rising sea-levels and worsening storms, the US is not imminently existentially threatened

---

[8] One can piece together much of this professional history from scattered references in *Climate Change and the Nation State*, which give the book a pleasing personal feel. Lieven's casual allusions to the impressive geographical range of his career also serve as a rhetorical demonstration of worldliness. Anecdotal experience is used to substantiate specific claims—his time in Qatar, for example, which 'has the most restrictive' naturalization laws in the world, convinced him of the incompatibility of a universal basic income with too much migration—and cumulatively, to empirically corroborate his 'realist' sensibility; his conclusions do not derive from ideological predilections, but arise organically from his wide experience: CCNS, pp. xvi–xvii, 49, 51, 132, 135.

by the physical consequences of a warming planet. Lieven's case for redefining climate change as a pressing national-security concern is thus founded on anticipating its socio-political fallout, rather than its immediate material effects, and on his elaboration of the ways in which, even if disastrous changes to the natural environment are relatively localized, their human and political consequences are not. The endangered world with which *Climate Change and the Nation State* is most concerned is thus not the natural one of forests and rivers and irreplaceable wildlife, but the political order of states and societies; the horizon upon which Lieven's gaze is fixed is not some ecological apocalypse or mass-extinction event, but the demise of democracies and societal collapse that he thinks will come first: without something like a Green New Deal, 'Western liberal democracies won't last long enough to be overwhelmed by the direct effects of climate change'.[9]

Lieven's appeal to 'securitize' the climate crisis touches on the aspect of the problem that can make it seem so hopelessly insoluble. While some countries have marshalled impressive resources and political will in response to the pandemic, the differences between the virus and climate change are suggestive. Unlike COVID-19, which rapidly spread to virtually every corner of the planet, the exact interaction between global warming and meteorological cycles, as with carbon emissions and their longer-term visible effects, is complex and contested, while impacts are uneven across regions and classes. As has widely been noted, the places most at risk from rising sea-levels, floods, storms, drought and other catastrophic natural events and processes, and least able to prepare for and recover from them, are mostly located in developing countries with little geopolitical clout, and whose national contribution to global emissions is negligible compared to many of the less vulnerable high-emitting countries.[10] Aside from its evident injustice, this asymmetry of cause and effect is also a serious obstacle to the mobilization of elites in the global North: whereas COVID-19 infected affluent globe-trotters first,

---

[9] CCNS, p. 115.

[10] The Philippines and Bangladesh, for example—3rd and 4th on HSBC's climate vulnerability ranking—were responsible for 0.35 per cent and 0.24 per cent of the 36.2 billion tonnes of carbon emitted in 2017 respectively. China and the US, meanwhile—ranked 26th and 39th by the HSBC report—emitted 27 per cent and 15 per cent of the global carbon total. See the visualization, 'Who emits the most CO2?' using data from the Global Carbon Project, in Hannah Ritchie and Max Roser, 'CO2 and Greenhouse Gas Emissions', May 2017, published at ourworldindata.org; and Ashim Paun, Lucy Acton and Wai-Shin Chan, 'Fragile Planet: Scoring Climate Risks Around the World', HSBC Global Research Report, March 2018.

including heads of state and their ministers, before percolating through lower-income and minority communities, over-represented in the service and care sectors and disproportionately killed by the virus, the last to be affected by climate change will likely be those with the most capacity but least immediate interest in mitigating it.

Lieven does not squarely acknowledge this dynamic, but it is implicitly conceded by the burden of his case, which is to square the circle of national and global interest by showing that climate change poses an 'indirect'—but immediate—existential threat to the West. The linchpin of Lieven's reconciliation of Western self-interest with planetary welfare—or rather, of the developing world's bearing on Western political calculation—is mass migration: 'the single most important threat posed by climate change to the security of the Western states and Russia is likely to be an indirect one: further increases in migration'.[11] There is evidence to suggest that Lieven's forecast of the mass displacement of populations is not scare-mongering. According to one recent report, with the desertification of semiarid regions, 'hundreds of millions of people from Central America to Sudan to the Mekong Delta' whose land has failed them 'will be forced to choose between flight and death. The result will almost certainly be the greatest wave of global migration the world has seen'. By 2070, the extremely hot zones that now account for less than 1 per cent of the earth's land surface could cover nearly a fifth of it, 'potentially placing one of every three people alive outside the climate niche where humans have thrived for thousands of years'.[12] Internal displacement, as rural communities deprived of their agricultural livelihoods move to cities in search of increasingly scarce waged work, and emigration to proximate countries will initially be more prevalent than intercontinental migration, which is often treacherous and requires a financial capacity that most lack.[13] But the scale of the crisis—'with every degree of temperature increase, roughly a billion' will be pushed outside

[11] CCNS, p. 35.
[12] Abrahm Lustgarten, 'The Great Climate Migration', New York Times Magazine, 26 July 2020.
[13] Of the roughly 13 million people displaced by the Syrian civil war—the 'refugee crisis' that Lieven repeatedly invokes to warn of the 'widespread populist radicalization and political destabilization' he believes rapid, mass migration to the West will inevitably cause—roughly half remained within Syria's borders, with a further 5 million displaced to neighbouring countries in the Middle East and North Africa, numbers which dwarf the 1 million who found asylum in Europe: Phillip Connor, 'Most Displaced Syrians Are in the Middle East', Pew Research Center, 29 January 2018.

the 'climate niche', and according to the UN global temperatures are on course to rise by as much as 3.9 degrees by 2100—suggests displacement will not be confined to the environs of impacted regions.[14]

Lieven foresees that the unprecedented magnitude and rapidity of this displacement will, alongside resource scarcity, exacerbate existing tensions, including ethnic conflicts, destabilizing whole regions, with many devolving into war, and potentially precipitating the collapse of states. 'Climate change will feed into other factors of environmental degradation and social tension, producing more conflicts like the Syrian civil war'—a conflict Lieven relates to the droughts in grain-growing countries in the years preceding it: he points to the steep rise in bread prices and ensuing economic discontent across the Middle East as an important context for the Arab Spring.[15] Mass migration, in other words, is Lieven's answer to the question of how, as Mike Davis puts it, to effect 'the transmutation of the self-interest of rich countries and classes into an enlightened "solidarity"' with the poorer countries and classes most vulnerable to the environmental devastation already being wrought by untrammelled energy use in the global North.[16]

Types of nationalism

Declaring the climate crisis a firm priority among security establishments is one tactic for focusing elite minds and neutralizing the issue among sceptical voters. But the larger, and more contentious, part of Lieven's scheme for turning climate-stabilization into a bipartisan popular cause is nationalism—'the most powerful source of collective effort in modern history'. *Climate Change and the Nation State* is in this sense a partial misnomer; *Climate Change and Nationalism* would be more accurate—though one can understand why Lieven preferred the former, since nationalism has, to put it mildly, a mixed reputation, as well as a highly uneven environmental record. Lieven acknowledges this, noting 'the melancholy examples' of Trump's enthusiastic rolling back of environmental regulations and Bolsonaro's commitment to hastening the deforestation of the Amazon. To impose some moral order on this protean ideology, Lieven makes the standard move of distinguishing

---

[14] Lustgarten, 'The Great Climate Migration'; Matt Stieb, '"Bleak" UN Climate Report: World on Track for Up to 3.9 Degrees Warming by 2100', *New York Magazine*, 26 November 2019.
[15] CCNS, pp. 36, 41.
[16] Mike Davis, 'Who Will Build the Ark?', NLR 61, Jan–Feb 2010, p. 37.

between ethnic and civic nationalisms: the former is 'an attempt at re-creating a state based on a narrow and closed ethnic and cultural identity'—which is 'obviously not desirable for any country containing large ethnic or religious minorities' and 'will in the end point toward fascism'—while the latter is 'based on a much stronger idea of common citizenship giving a common sense of identity to all citizens', irrespective of race or creed.[17]

Lieven draws on myriad historical examples to attest the progressive achievements of nationalism but is most inspired by the 'social imperialists' of Western Europe at the turn of the 20th century and Theodore Roosevelt's Progressive movement in the US, both of which, in Lieven's telling, successfully combined patriotism with welfarism. Lieven, whose electoralist horizon means he conceives of the durable popularity required to forge a new, eco-friendly national consensus as an artefact of bipartisanship achieved through a kind of depoliticization, is perhaps also attracted to the ecumenical politics of the British social imperialists: they were 'drawn mainly from the imperialist wing of the Liberal Party' but included 'Fabian socialists' and '"one nation" Conservatives', as well as 'the more farsighted sections of the military elites'. What united this 'eclectic bunch' was an enthusiasm for Empire, anticipation of a 'coming world war in which national unity would be tested to the limit', 'professional middle-class contempt' for Britain's aristocratic ruling class, and a 'deep fear of revolution, class warfare, and social disintegration'. To either forestall or prepare for these multiple threats, the social imperialists believed the British state 'needed to be thoroughly reformed and given increased powers, including to shape and guide the economy'; their vision 'extended beyond social insurance to urban planning, public health, and educational reform'. Despite plunging the Continent into the First World War, and regrettable 'parallels with the European tendencies that contributed to fascism' after it, 'the social imperialists contributed to the growing national consensus that eventually created the British welfare state after 1945'. Today's 'task' is thus 'to develop a new version of social imperialism without the imperialism, racism, eugenics, and militarism'. In the US the same mix of progressive taxation, a more energetic and compassionate state, and pride in one's country animated Theodore Roosevelt's 'new Nationalism', the 1912 platform of the fleeting Progressive Party. This beneficent form of nationalism helped to create basic social welfare, regulating 'the wild

[17] CCNS, pp. xv, 84–5.

capitalism of the "Gilded Age"'—attacking 'the power of special interests and monopolies' and holding executives 'personally responsible for the crimes of their corporations'—and modernizing government.[18]

How convincing a strategy is Lieven's counter-intuitive call to recast the planetary crisis in nationalist terms? Its presupposition—that nation-states 'are not going away', and are the only agents with the legitimacy and resources to respond at the speed and scale required to stabilize the climate—seems increasingly self-evident, notwithstanding their inertia on climate action to date and the globalized nature of the climate activist movement. Intergovernmental bodies—from the UN's IPCC to the WHO—can issue warnings and guidance, arrange conferences and aggregate expertise, and perhaps in some cases exert pressure; but without territorial sovereignty or democratic legitimacy, they are comparatively powerless to act or compel action. As for the traditional alternative to the state—the market—even the *Economist* admits that its invisible hand is not up to the task of spontaneously decarbonizing the economy in time.[19]

Lieven's delineation of the theoretical fit between nationalism and environmentalism is often compelling. 'If climate change and other challenges are to be met, then the states of the 21st century will have to be strong', Lieven contends, and the 'greatest source of a state's strength is not its economy or the size of its armed forces, but legitimacy in the eyes of its population'. There are various sources of state legitimacy—from sheer longevity to administrative competency—but one of the 'greatest and most enduring' has been nationalism. By fortifying and legitimizing states, nationalism eases the implementation of 'painful reforms' and demands for collective sacrifice—in the form of higher taxes, including unpopular fuel levies, which Lieven believes will be a necessary part of greening the economy.[20] Nationalism is also, Lieven argues, predicated on a concern for the future and so ready-made for the 'long-term thinking' required for climate action: unlike its ephemeral individual citizens,

---

[18] CCNS, pp. 96–101.
[19] Whereas past energy transitions were slow—'it was not until the 1950s, a century after the first commercial oil well was drilled' in Pennsylvania that 'crude oil came to represent 25 per cent of humankind's total primary energy'—the switch to cleaner energy sources needs to happen improbably fast. 'Private capital will follow' public policy, but governments 'need to make the signals clear': 'Not-so-slow burn', *Economist*, 23 May 2020, pp. 53–4.
[20] CCNS, p. 76.

permanence is constitutive of the idea of a nation. Since it draws on an attachment to place—to local landscapes and heritage—nationalism is well suited to conservation efforts too.

But aside from these thought-provoking affinities, what does Lieven's 'civic' nationalism amount to in practice? In his final chapter, 'The Green New Deal and National Solidarity', Lieven turns his attention to the optics of actually existing green programmes in Europe and the US. Other than briefly lambasting the French Green Party for advocating the abandonment of nuclear energy—which he regards as wildly irresponsible based on a comparison of the lethality of runaway climate change versus a nuclear accident ('at least nine *million* human beings die every year as a direct result of air pollution'; '*Nobody* died as an immediate result of the Fukushima accident')—Lieven's main criticism of the French Greens is their stance on migration, which Lieven claims all European Green parties share. 'Since elsewhere in the party manifesto there is a call for the distinction between asylum seekers and economic migrants to be abolished', their pro-asylum policy 'is in effect a call for open borders. Such a programme would tear France apart'.[21] Note that Lieven makes his case against what he construes as hazardously liberal migration policies on impeccably ecological grounds: climate change will cause mass migration, and the arrival of millions fleeing the heat will in turn make taking action to mitigate climate change more difficult by increasing 'populist chauvinism'—a synonym for the malign 'ethnic' nationalism Lieven is keen to distinguish from his progressive 'civic' kind—'political radicalization, polarization, and state paralysis in Western democracies'. Lieven argues that as electorates become more deeply divided and ecologically obtuse far-right populists surge, the stable parliamentary majorities necessary for sustained government action on climate change will become a 'mathematical impossibility'.

Lieven reckons that if 'migration to the West can be kept within reasonable limits, and without sudden massive spikes like the Syrian refugee crisis', then 'there is a good chance' migrants can be 'successfully integrated', but worries that too much migration too fast will undermine the social cohesion he thinks will be vital for the acceptance of unpopular ecological reforms and state resilience in the face of worsening climate-related traumas.[22] The latter argument is predicated on the

---

[21] CCNS, pp. 117–8.
[22] CCNS, p. 56. Lieven doesn't specify what these 'reasonable limits' would be, nor does he spell out the optimal criteria for assessing asylum claims.

idea—derived from David Goodhart, whose *The British Dream* (2013) appears frequently in the footnotes of *Climate Change and the Nation State*—that stable societies with functioning and generous welfare states tend to be relatively culturally homogeneous, and that influxes of foreigners undermine social solidarity and with it, citizens' willingness to contribute taxes to support public services and fund green infrastructure, or to make sacrifices on behalf of the wider community, including its future generations.

Valences of migration

Lieven's vision of divided and paralysed democracies involves a strangely unmediated conception of the relation between migration and its political upshot. 'The continued flow of illegal immigration to the United States', he writes, has done 'much to infuriate sections of the white population and to elect Donald Trump.' Or: 'The result of mass migration in the generation before 2016 was the disaster of Brexit.'[23] Omitted in these analyses of 2016's political shocks is the way ideas about migration—ideas, moreover, that are not simply naturally arising, but deliberately propagated and instrumentalized for particular ends—condition people's reaction to it.[24] In step with Lieven's elision of what might be termed the ideological field, in which understandings of experience and material reality are always partly defined and constructed, is an equivocation in his analysis of the social and economic impact of mass migration, which, he argues, will—in combination with 'two other critical challenges for Western societies: automation and artificial intelligence'—wrack labour markets. Discussing the possible inclusion of a universal basic income (UBI) in green platforms, Lieven couches his claims that this would be at odds with 'open' migration policies in a kind of intellectual ventriloquy of the anti-immigrant perspective. A UBI would be 'incompatible with continued high levels of migration' not necessarily because migrants put a strain on the public purse—the evidence suggests they make a net fiscal contribution—but because a UBI would allow citizens to calculate the exact cost of migration: 'fears about added strains on social welfare, health, housing, and school systems have been among the chief causes of opposition to migration' but 'the evidence for

---

[23] CCNS, pp. 24, 60.
[24] For an alternative, see Maya Goodfellow: 'The disinclination to confront myths, and indeed the eagerness to reinforce them, cultivated anti-immigration politics in the UK and would ultimately help to produce the Brexit vote', *Hostile Environment: How Immigrants Became Scapegoats*, London and New York 2020, p. 8.

these costs has always been somewhat difficult to pin down', whereas 'under a UBI system', 'anyone with a pocket calculator could work out how much his or her basic income would drop for every given new percentage of migrants'.[25]

Is a UBI incompatible with high levels of migration because migrants really do stretch states' welfare capacities, or is the salient fact just that many voters believe this to be so? Likewise, should green parties adopt a more stringent position on migration because migrants destabilize societies and incapacitate political systems—thus impeding concerted action to address one of the causes of such migration—or simply because pro-asylum policies are bound to alienate right-wing voters? It is on account of this equivocation that one is left with the feeling that the historically informed defence of nationalism that constitutes much of the body of *Climate Change and the Nation State* is merely a theoretical embellishment of the Machiavellian electoral calculation with which it ends. This impression is reinforced by Lieven's discussion of the Democrats' 2019 Green New Deal Resolution too, where his larger theme of how to unleash the progressive ecological potential of nationalism tapers off into the rather less impressive, if still important, question of how to sell the Green New Deal to Republicans, which in turn seems at times to morph into the more cynical question of how to instrumentalize jingoistic and racist habits for environmental ends. For as Lieven does not shy away from saying: the irony of the right's climate-denial and ardent fossil-fuel consumption is that it is helping to precipitate the waves of migration they so detest and fear; their xenophobia alone should convert them to the planetary cause.

Referring to the wording of their GND Resolution, Lieven writes that 'the Democrats cannot afford to be tainted by the atmosphere of blanket hatred of core American traditions that suffuses their most radical supporters.' He doesn't elaborate on what these 'core American traditions' are—such indeterminacy enhances the euphemistic force of the phrase—but goes on to lament the way 'the resolution is framed in the language of "Green Intersectionality"' and then quotes the offending passage: climate change has 'exacerbated systemic racial, regional, social, environmental, and economic injustices' by 'disproportionately affecting indigenous peoples, communities of colour, migrant communities, deindustrialized communities, depopulated rural communities, the poor, low-income workers, women, the elderly, the unhoused, people with disabilities, and youth'. Lieven goes on to say that intersectionality downplays social and economic (as opposed to sexual and racial) disadvantage and so classes 'the most economically and socially disadvantaged white males among the privileged oppressors'. 'Why, for example, did the resolution have to slip in a completely gratuitous (and in spirit, mendacious) insult to the white working classes by claiming "a difference of 20 times more wealth between the average white family and the average black family"?' 'This sort of language is politically disastrous because it gives yet more opportunities to the Republicans to tell white working-class voters that the Democrats are not interested in them.' Lieven then claims that these 'hard-line cultural liberal positions' are 'not even popular with most Democrats' and uses a 2018 poll about political correctness to substantiate his point: 'almost 80 per cent of both blacks and whites in the United States dislike political correctness'.

'Of course', Lieven goes on, 'Democrats have a civic duty genuinely to *help* minorities who will vote for them anyway or not vote at all, but they need to pitch their electoral appeal to public voters who will *not* vote for them without considerable effort.' 'Climate change activism', he concludes, 'has become associated with the cultural liberals' sacralization of different ethnic and cultural identities and gratuitous attacks on conservative cultural symbols in recent decades, and this has necessarily alienated conservatives who might otherwise have recognized the threat of climate change to their nations.'[26] Here, Lieven's carefully defined civic nationalism seems heedlessly to slide into meaning something quite different. As with 'core American traditions', Lieven doesn't explain what he means by 'conservative cultural symbols', but the strong implication is that the symbols and traditions that are being 'attacked' or 'insulted' by allusion to the way ethnicity inflects class inequalities are specifically white. This closing descent into a discussion that has the feel of a rant undoes Lieven's carefully prepared distinction between the inclusionary, acceptable, progressive kind of nationalism and its reactionary, racist counterpart.

But if *Climate Change and the Nation State*'s crescendo is morally weak, it is also strategically underwhelming. Given the heterogeneity of the contemporary working class, the sociological or empirical basis of Lieven's 'realism'—and his impatience with any references to communities of

---

[26] CCNS, pp. 129–32.

colour, migrants, women and so on as impolitic 'fetishization of identity politics'—seems questionable.[27] Moreover, despite Lieven's thoughtful, often persuasive tracing of the ideological overlap between nationalism and environmentalism, his central recommendations are decidedly cosmetic, confined to the level of discourse.[28] To 'securitize' the climate crisis, for example, Lieven advocates 'strong public recognition by the military of the threat of climate change to the United States', or what he calls 'a speech act in the area of security'.[29] Such discursive shifts are not without material power, of course—Lieven's Austinian term 'speech act' suggests as much—but, as with his urging the omission of divisive stances on migration and racism, they can seem a rather thin basis upon which to pin one's hopes for the planet.

Lieven's characterization of the GND Resolution's mention of race as 'political correctness'—as if, again, to ventriloquize a right-wing retort—also suggests a shaky intellectual grasp of this position. To carry off the mediatory role between 'cultural liberals' and conservatives in which Lieven casts himself requires an understanding of the nuance of, and differentiation within, each side's perspective. This means avoiding caricature or treating fringe positions as if they are representative. The 'idea of a borderless state with a completely open identity', as Lieven puts it, has libertarian supporters on both the left and the right, but it is not the position of the Congressional Democrats who proposed the Green New Deal. Sanders, for example, is committed to an immediate moratorium on deportations; reuniting families, reinstating and expanding DACA; and welcoming refugees and asylum seekers, including those displaced by climate change. *Mutatis mutandis*, Corbyn's policies were similarly reformist; *Climate Change and the Nation State* doesn't indicate which of these demands should be dropped to attract anti-immigrant voters. But Lieven's reductive approach extends beyond the thorny question of migration: he at one point suggests that 'most Greens' are opposed 'to even researching' 'carbon removal' because 'this would remove one argument for the elimination of capitalism'.[30] Some eco-socialists may harbour suspicions about technological fixes, but the idea that 'most Greens' would be against exploring any solutions that would obviate

---

[27] CCNS, p. 57.
[28] A scattering of more substantial policy preferences emerges from the book—a 'small tax on financial transactions rigorously enforced', 'much higher fuel prices', 'tough action to raise money from the elites', including stamping out tax evasion and stricter regulation of the banks—but these are incidental to its main argument.
[29] CCNS, p. 7.   [30] CCNS, p. 120.

the need for more fundamental political change—i.e., that solicitude for the planet is merely an indifferent instrument for furthering an anti-capitalist agenda—strains credulity. Lieven's exegesis of the Democrats' GND Resolution is similarly hyperbolic. Its 'sacralization of different ethnic and cultural identities' is a minor part of the text: mention of the 'racial wealth divide' and 'gender earnings gap' are bottom of a long list of 'related crises', topped by declining life expectancy, stagnant wages, low socio-economic mobility, the erosion of workers' bargaining power, income inequality and so on. Lieven wishes Democrats would talk of 'elite privilege' or 'corporate privilege' instead of 'white privilege', but the phrase 'communities of colour' appears only twice in the Resolution, while 'worker' is mentioned eleven times.[31] Lieven understands himself to be presenting a challenge to the ecologically concerned left who can't get their priorities straight—or as Adam Tooze parses the now-overfa-miliar provocation: 'Will we sacrifice our ideological hobby-horses for the sake of doing whatever it takes to prevent climate catastrophe?'[32] But some of Lieven's claims about the left's positions give one reason to doubt this self-understanding—that is, to wonder whether Lieven is really posing the question, or challenge, he thinks and says he is.

All 'realists' to some extent circumscribe the reality to which their 'realism' corresponds—that is, a 'realist case' rests on a prior defi-nition of what 'being realistic' is. To Lieven, the reality is that taking action to mitigate climate change means GND-supporting political parties winning repeated national elections. Few would dispute the legitimacy of this electoralist framework given the urgency of the cir-cumstances—2030, by which time, according to the Democrats' GND Resolution, carbon emissions need to be down by 40 per cent, is only a couple of presidential terms away—but others of Lieven's 'givens' are more open to question. His unmediated conception of the relation-ship between the fact of migration and the prevalence or virulence of xenophobia, for example, suggests an exaggerated sense of the fixity of ideas—the implication is that the only way to overcome anti-immigrant sentiment, presumed to be an inevitable reaction to the presence of migrants, is to reduce migration. This overrating of the permanence of ideas—an aspect of the elision of the ideological field—is paradoxi-cally dependent on an under-estimation of the material conditions in

---

[31] The text of the Resolution 'recognizing the duty of the Federal Government to create a Green New Deal' is available at congress.gov.
[32] Adam Tooze, 'Politics for the End of the World', *New Statesman*, 1 April 2020.

which they take hold. For in the same way that climate denialism is not merely a conservative cultural habit formed in reaction to loud liberal moralizing about capitalism's destructive plundering of the planet's resources, but the result of determined and well-resourced campaigns by fossil-fuel companies and their lobbyists, antipathy is not a spontaneous response to migration but partly an ideological reaction to wider material circumstances—economic insecurity, for example—as well as to the top-down dissemination and validation of such ideas.[33]

A warming globe and mass migration may be intractable facts about our future, but is hostility to migrants a similarly inevitable aspect of pre-political reality? As Stuart Hall wrote following Labour's general election defeat in 1987, 'Politics does not reflect majorities, it constructs them.'[34] Lieven's strategy is in some ways a call for a more class-based politics rooted in the social ruins left by 'free-market capitalism run amok', which Lieven thinks presents an electoral opportunity: 'The growing immiseration of large sections of the white working classes is opening up important new political possibilities across racial lines—if the Democrats know how to use them.'[35] Yet a spirit of togetherness achieved through appealing to a sense of nationhood that tactfully avoids acknowledging the existence of heterogeneity seems a rather shallow attempt to reflect perceived majorities, rather than to construct a more durable unity, grounded in the recognition of the diversity of experience.

The rhetorical function of Lieven's self-described 'realism' is to present his arguments as derived from an unblinking confrontation with the facts, unencumbered by anything as compromising and impractical as ideological commitment or moral priorities. The same goes for the way the neat reciprocity of his case against mass migration—climate change causes mass migration, which hinders political efforts to address climate change—skirts moral questions. But notwithstanding this siphoning off of such 'extraneous' concerns from strategic ones in the name of realism, one can still ask: what are the moral consequences of Lieven's strategy, or to what ends does its logic point? Posing this question about whether nationalism is an appropriate or acceptable ideological

---

[33] Lieven does pay lip-service to 'the power and determination of opposition to reform from the banking and energy sectors' on a couple of occasions, but this passing acknowledgement does not essentially inform his analysis of the current deadlock, nor his strategy for overcoming it: CCNS, pp. 105, xiv.
[34] Stuart Hall, 'Blue Election, Election Blues', Marxism Today, July 1987.
[35] CCNS, p. 134.

instrument for popularizing the Green New Deal reveals a weakness in Lieven's conception of nationalism, which could be summarized as excessively voluntaristic.

One can observe the influence of Tom Nairn—whom Lieven cites as one of the 'leading thinkers who have helped to inspire this book'— in Lieven's conviction that nationalism can be a positive, modernizing force. In Nairn's sophisticated, humane characterization in 'The Modern Janus', nationalism appears as a beleaguered and defensive ideology, but also as resourceful, and animated by a will to survive that is propulsive, life-affirming and future-oriented rather than nihilistic. But whereas Nairn's nationalism appears, above all, as a natural phenomenon, analogous to pathology in individuals—this is what makes his insistence on its moral and political ambiguity so convincing—Lieven's version of nationalism is improbably deliberate: 'the *choice* then is between stupid, short-sighted versions of nationalism and intelligent, far-sighted ones'.[36] This means that he does not properly account for the possibility that once nationalism's formal force has been summoned, its content may not be 'controllable', as Nairn puts it: 'In the social trauma as in the individual one, once these well-springs have been tapped there is no real guarantee that the great forces will be "controllable" (in the sense of doing only what they are supposed to do, and no more)'.[37]

Lieven does not address the possibility—the likelihood even, given the *prima facie* solipsism of nationalism—that, as Mike Davis writes:

> growing environmental and socio-economic turbulence may simply drive elite publics into more frenzied attempts to wall themselves off from the rest of humanity. Global mitigation, in this unexplored but not improbable scenario, would be tacitly abandoned—as, to some extent, it already has been—in favour of accelerated investment in selective adaptation for Earth's first-class passengers. The goal would be the creation of green and gated oases of permanent affluence on an otherwise stricken planet.

The 'transmutation of the self-interest of rich countries and classes into an enlightened solidarity"' only seems realistic, Davis continues, if it can be shown 'that greenhouse gas mitigation can be achieved without major sacrifices in northern hemispheric standards of living'.[38] Defining

---

[36] CCNS, p. xvi. My emphasis.
[37] Tom Nairn, 'The Modern Janus', NLR I/94, Nov–Dec 1975, pp. 17, 19.
[38] Davis, 'Who Will Build the Ark?', pp. 37–8.

the climate crisis as a national security threat in the West does not solve the problem of how to prevail upon elites to impose sacrifices on their own populations on behalf of those residing beyond their borders; it circumvents it. Indeed, part of the substance of Lieven's 'realism' rests on the grim calculus that it is only as a threat to Western stability that electorates and elites can be convinced to behave *as if* they care about others' plight. But once solidarity and altruism have been wholly discarded as principles of action, what can guarantee that this accidental collision of self-interest and Other-interest will endure?

Exploiting the anti-immigrant backlash with which contemporary forms of nationalism seem so entwined for the sake of the planet may swing some voters, but likely in both directions; and what might the human cost of this electoral strategy be for the populations who are already fleeing or will need to flee even if we reach net-zero by 2050? *Climate Change and the Nation State* is useful for its broad reminder that building political coalitions means finding ways to communicate with the unconverted, and that the case for an egalitarian green stimulus programme is not universally self-evident but needs making with strategic intelligence. The challenge, however, is to devise alternative senses of what 'being realistic' is by forging new expectations about what reality can and should be like—to redefine 'commonsense', not tailor GND PR to its existing, pernicious forms. Moreover, given that much of the heating predicted by climate scientists in the coming decades is not preventable but guaranteed, domestic reform to mitigate climate change in the high-emitting countries of the global North—through eradicating fossil fuels, expanding clean transportation networks, improving agricultural practices, retrofitting homes and so on—needs to happen in combination with adaptation, including migration and development policies that do not trap impoverished populations in unliveable regions, whether this is *sensu stricto* in their 'national' interest or not.

STANFORD UNIVERSITY PRESS

Oilcraft
*The Myths of
Scarcity and
Security That
Haunt U.S.
Energy Policy*
Robert Vitalis

Queer Alliances
*How Power
Shapes Political
Movement
Formation*
Erin Mayo-Adam

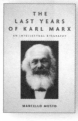

**The Last Years
of Karl Marx**
*An Intellectual
Biography*
Marcello Musto

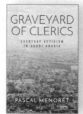

**Graveyard
of Clerics**
*Everyday Activism
in Saudi Arabia*
Pascal Menoret

**Tyranny
of Greed**
*Trump,
Corruption, and
the Revolution
to Come*
Timothy K.
Kuhner

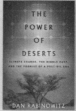

**The Power
of Deserts**
*Climate Change,
the Middle East,
and the Promise
of a Post-Oil Era*
Dan Rabinowitz

STANFORD BRIEFS

 sup.org
stanfordpress.typepad.com

NEW Open Access titles from UCL Press

Community-Led Regeneration
A Toolkit for Residents and Planners
Pablo Sendra and Daniel Fitzpatrick

"Described as a "toolkit for residents and planners", this is no dry theoretical survey, but a practical guide for the thousands of people currently facing uncertainty about the future of their homes... bringing activists together to share their experiences and build a collective body of knowledge that will be so important for future campaigns." Oliver Wainwright, The Guardian

April 2020 184 pages 9781787356061
Open Access https://www.uclpress.co.uk/products/125696
Also available in hbk & pbk £40/ £20

Refuge in a Moving World
Tracing refugee and migrant journeys across disciplines
Edited by Elena Fiddian-Qasmiyeh

Refuge in a Moving World draws together more than thirty contributions from multiple disciplines and fields of research and practice to discuss different ways of engaging with, and responding to, migration and displacement.

July 2020 566 pages 9781787353176
Open Access https://www.uclpress.co.uk/products/116728
Also available in hbk & pbk £45/ £30

Restaging the Past
Historical Pageants, Culture and Society in Modern Britain
Edited by Angela Bartie, Linda Fleming, Mark Freeman, Alexander Hutton, and Paul Readman

Historical pageants began as an Edwardian craze, but persisted as important events in communities and organizations across Britain for much of the next hundred years. Taken together, they represent one of the most significant aspects of popular engagement with the past in twentieth-century Britain – this is the first book devoted to their study.

August 2020 244 pages 9781787354050
Open Access https://www.uclpress.co.uk/products/123496
Also available in hbk & pbk £45/ £25

Heritage Futures
Comparative Approaches to Natural and Cultural Heritage Practices
Rodney Harrison, Caitlin DeSilvey, Cornelius Holtorf, Sharon Macdonald, Nadia Bartolini, Esther Breithoff, Harald Fredheim, Antony Lyons, Sarah May, Jennie Morgan, and Sefryn Penrose

Heritage Futures draws on research undertaken over four years by an interdisciplinary, international team of 16 researchers and more than 25 partner organisations to explore the role of heritage and heritage-like practices in building future worlds.

July 2020 568 pages 9781787356009
Open Access https://www.uclpress.co.uk/products/125034
Also available in hbk & pbk £50/ £35

To download all of our titles open access go to **www.uclpress.co.uk**

 @uclpress @uclpress

UCLPRESS

GÖRAN THERBORN

DREAMS AND NIGHTMARES

OF THE WORLD'S MIDDLE CLASSES

T HE WORLD HAS been getting contradictory messages about
its class structure. According to one authoritative account, it
has reached a 'global tipping point'—'half the world is now
middle class or wealthier'. This was based on figures marshalled by Homi Kharas, a former World Bank chief economist now at
Brookings. More excitably, the *Economist* has hailed the 'relentless rise'
of a 'burgeoning bourgeoisie' and trumpeted the arrival of a middle-class
world. Yet serious scholarship also assures us of the opposite: according
to Peter Temin, emeritus professor of economics at MIT, we should be
concerned about 'the vanishing middle class'.[1] Readers could be forgiven
for feeling bewildered. What is going on in economics—and in the economic sociology of the real world? This contribution will examine the
varying definitions of 'middle class' in play and the contrasting trajectories analysed by development economists, sociologists and financial
journalists across the different sectors of the world economy. It will go
on to outline a rather different future for the world's middle classes than
either of the extremes suggested here. But first, a few historical and conceptual considerations may be in order, for the concept of the 'middle
class' has long given rise to debate.

The term 'middle class' entered the English language two centuries ago—
'sometime between 1790 and 1830', according to Eric Hobsbawm—as
a rising industrial society overtook the 'military' order of monarchy
and aristocracy.[2] The nineteenth century saw intensive discussion over
where this new society was headed and the place of the middle class
within it. The liberal argument was that the task of government should,
and would, fall to the middle class, 'the most wise and the most virtuous

part of the community', as James Mill put it.[3] Had this already been accomplished? For Tocqueville, writing in 1855, the reign of the middle class had been realized not only in the United States but also in France, where the July Revolution of 1830 marked its 'definitive' and 'complete' triumph.[4] Would the emergent middle-class society lead on to a new and stable political order? In the later decades of the nineteenth century, this was increasingly questioned. Novel 'isms' appeared: mobilizing ideas, first and foremost socialism, which theorized 'middle-class society' as capitalism, doomed to be overthrown by the expanded ranks of the industrial working class.

Middle class and bourgeoisie

Most strikingly, nineteenth-century discussions featured a conceptual variety notably absent from current treatments of the 'middle class'. This derived from the flourishing of a number of national languages, each expressing a particular history of class formation and conflict. In Western Europe, there were three major concepts circling around a similar social phenomenon, each from a different angle: the English 'middle class' was complemented by the German *Bürgertum* and French *bourgeoisie*.[5] Both originated in medieval urban law, denoting a category of urban residents with special civic and political rights. After the French Revolution, the 'bourgeoisie' grew increasingly synonymous with both the English 'middle class' and the *classe(s) moyenne(s)*. But it also took on two distinct connotations. One was culturally pejorative: as Flaubert put it, 'Hatred of the bourgeois is the beginning of all virtue.'[6] Second,

---

[1] Homi Kharas and Kristofer Hamel, 'A Global Tipping Point: Half the World is Now Middle Class or Wealthier', Brookings Future Development Blog, 27 September 2018; 'Burgeoning Bourgeoisie', *Economist*, 14 February 2009; Peter Temin, *The Vanishing Middle Class*, Cambridge MA, 2017.

[2] Eric Hobsbawm, 'Die Englische Middle Class, 1780–1830', in Jürgen Kocka, ed., *Bürgertum im 19. Jahrhundert*, vol. 1, Munich 1988, p. 79.

[3] James Mill, 'Essay on Government' [1829], quoted from Hobsbawm, 'Die Englische Middle Class', p. 81. Mill's view of the wisdom and virtue of the middle class is still echoed by development economists and political scientists today, as if those classes had given no backing to fascism and military dictatorships in the interval.

[4] Alexis de Tocqueville, *Souvenirs* [1855], cited from Peter Gay, *Schnitzler's Century*, New York 2002, p. 14. Latter-day historians have tended to agree that the power and privileges of the landowning aristocracy persisted in most of Europe down to 1914: Arno Meyer, *The Persistence of the Old Regime*, New York 1981.

[5] For further details, see the important research project directed by Jürgen Kocka, *Bürgertum im 19. Jahrhundert*, 3 vols, Munich 1988.

[6] Letter to George Sand, here quoted from Gay, *Schnitzler's Century*, p. 29.

from the 1870s a clear distinction arose between the bourgeoisie and the 'middle' or 'new' social strata. The bourgeoisie were the big capital owners: bankers and industrialists, the new peak of the social pyramid—that is to say, the upper class.[7] The middle class—the German *Mittelstand*; the *petite bourgeoisie* or *couches moyennes* in French—was something different. In the *Communist Manifesto* Marx and Engels paid handsome tribute to the 'revolutionary' historical role played by the bourgeoisie, now seen as the embodiment of capital and the sworn enemy of the working class.

Another noteworthy difference: work was a crucial attribute and value of the nineteenth-century middle class, the thing that separated it from the rent-consuming nobility. 'Work is the burgher's ornament', wrote Friedrich Schiller in a famous ballad. 'Blessed is he who has found his work, let him ask no other blessedness', added Thomas Carlyle in *Past and Present*.[8] In today's discussions, the middle class is overwhelmingly defined in terms of consumption, or rather consumer capacity, measured in dollars (as corrected by international purchasing power parities); occasionally it is specified by some middling location on the national ladder of income distribution—but never by reference to its work. This is all the more remarkable, since contemporary American usage typically deploys the term as a euphemism for the working class.

What are the implications of this mutation of middle-class discourse, from work to consumption? The *Economist*'s enthusiastic hailing of another 'two billion bourgeois' offers a clue.[9] Like the entry of 'capitalism' into the vocabulary of business executives, it is a celebration of victory and power. So long as socialism was seen as a danger, terms like 'capitalism' and 'the bourgeoisie' were banished to the margins; the acceptable terms were 'market economy' and 'business'. As we shall see, the discursive change connotes an important shift in social hegemony. But first we should examine the conditions that gave rise to the twenty-first century's new thinking on the middle class.

Contra Mill and Tocqueville, the nineteenth century did not usher in a middle-class world, for the twentieth century was above all defined by the

---

[7] Adeline Daumard, *Les bourgeois et la bourgeoisie en France*, Paris 1987. The transition is indicated by the *Petit Robert* dictionary: a bourgeois is one 'who belongs to the middle and ruling'—*moyenne et dirigeante*—'or just to the ruling class'.
[8] Gay, *Schnitzler's Century*, p. 192.
[9] 'Two Billion More Bourgeois', *Economist*, 14 February 2009.

working class. Although social democracy and communism were born in Europe, working-class socialism became a world model, conspicuous in the Chinese and the Vietnamese revolutions, with their repercussions throughout East and Southeast Asia; in revolutionary Mexico and Fidelista Cuba; in the large progressive movements of Latin America— Peronist Argentina and Vargas's Brazil, not to mention the PT of more recent times—and in anti-colonial struggles, from Nehru's Congress via Arab socialism to the ANC of South Africa. The labour movement was a major force in the achievement of universal suffrage and the welfare state. It was the main ally—although seldom an exemplary one—of the feminist and anti-imperialist movements. The middle classes were largely in hibernation through these twentieth-century periods of revolution and reform; they gained political salience at times of rising fascism and authoritarianism. But the motor force of working-class reform peaked in the years around 1980 and then rapidly declined.

The end of the working-class century had an economic basis in the accelerating deindustrialization and financialization of the capitalist core; more obliquely, a sociological factor was the social dissolution stemming from the 1968 cultural movement. Yet this did not immediately herald a new middle-class dawn. Western neoliberalism was allergic to any kind of class discourse, and Eastern European anti-Communists preferred to refer to themselves as 'civil society', although in power they would claim middle-class credentials.[10] If, as Hobsbawm thought, the idea of the middle class was born in the West, it was reborn in the East and the South.[11] In the 1980s the middle class was 'discovered' in conservative East Asia, as an outcome of the rapid economic growth of the 'four little dragons': Taiwan, South Korea, Singapore, Hong Kong.[12] The middle classes were emerging as a significant political force in the region, playing central roles in the broad popular movements that put an end to military dictatorships in Seoul and Taipei.

In China, the concept travelled a rockier path to acceptance. In the 1980s, Chinese academic interest in the middle class was in part inspired by the

[10] A line-drawing sociological conference was held in Bulgaria in 1998: Nikolai Tilkidjiev, ed., The Middle Class as a Precondition of a Sustainable Society, Sofia 1998.
[11] Cf. Marcus Gräser, '"The Great Middle Class" in the Nineteenth-Century United States', in Christof Dejung, David Motadel and Jürgen Osterhammel, eds, The Global Bourgeoisie, Princeton 2019.
[12] Its 'discovery' was the work of the East Asia Middle Class Project of Academica Sinica in Taiwan. See Hsin-Huang Michael Hsiao, ed., Discovery of the Middle Classes in East Asia, Taipei 1993.

American neo-Marxism of Erik Olin Wright and his colleagues. After 1989, following Tiananmen, government orthodoxy hit back. A prominent line-following sociologist put it this way: socialist China could not allow a 'middle class' to appear, since this could 'overturn our socialist system'. Whereas middle-class theory in the West 'exists to cover up the issue of class conflict', in socialist societies it 'divides the proletariat, separating businesspeople and intellectuals from the proletariat, creating a subversive force.' After a period of silence, however, the middle-class discussion reopened, and from 2001 the debate was won decisively by the argument that 'in any society, the middle class is the most important force in maintaining social stability'—a cushion between the upper and the lower classes, the bearer of moderate and conservative ideologies, and the crux of a broad and stable consumer market.[13] To many Chinese scholars in the 2000s the middle class also became an egalitarian ideal, the key to an 'olive-shaped' social structure.[14] Vietnam's post-Communist conceptual change was encapsulated by the Deputy Prime Minister, Hoàng Trung Hải. 'The young middle-class population will be the driving force in Asia', Hải declared, referring to 'the arrival of a billion more middle-class consumers'. Thirty years earlier, his predecessor would have referred to the working class as the 'driving force'.[15]

I. SOUTHERN DREAMS

The new middle-class dream in the Global South had, first and foremost, an Asian setting. It was woven and promoted by figures in the World Bank's orbit, seconded by business consultancies and investment bankers. It appeared at the start of the millennium, the *belle époque* of outsourced global capitalism. As noted above, the Eastern rediscovery of the middle class in the 1980s was made by sociologists, concerned with changing occupational structures and class formations, and interested in their social and political implications. The new triumphalism, by contrast, was almost exclusively about consumption. 'Middle class' meant anybody who had some money to spend. By the same token, it soon came to mean being non-poor, as defined by official national poverty

---

[13] The narrative and quotations are derived from Li Chunling, 'Changes in Theoretical Directions and Interests of Research on China's Middle Class', in Li, ed., *The Rising Middle Classes and China*, Beijing 2012, pp. 6–8.
[14] Jean-Louis Rocca, 'Political Crossroad, Social Transformation and Academic Intervention: The Formation of the Middle Class in China', in Li, *The Rising Middle Classes and China*, p. 36. Cf. Li, 'Changes in Theoretical Directions', p. 8.
[15] Hai was speaking at the 2009 World Economic Forum in East Asia.

lines.[16] The notion of a middle class that began just above the poorest 20 per cent of the population—who, in poor countries, tend to be very poor indeed—was bolstered in 2000 by an influential paper from William Easterly, a tough-minded Hayekian then at the World Bank. In 'The Middle-Class Consensus and Economic Development', Easterly argued that the inequality represented by the (low) income share of the three middle quintiles of the population—which he dubbed the 'middle class', without any supporting arguments—was a hindrance to development.[17] Middle-class expansion therefore became synonymous with the decline of poverty—a conceptual linkage that connected the concerns of development economists about poverty reduction with the interests of business consultants hunting for new markets.

Rising Asia

Indeed, it was US business consultants and bankers who first started to big-up the Asian middle-class dream. In 2007, McKinsey predicted that middle-class Indian consumers would grow from 50 million to 583 million by 2025. The following year, Goldman Sachs foresaw global inequality tumbling thanks to the 'exploding world middle class'.[18] The *Economist* was tail-ending this boosterism with its claim of 'two billion more bourgeois'. The first major quantitative overview of the 'bulging' middle class appeared in January 2009, authored by World Bank economist Martin Ravallion. It defined 'middle class' as living on $2–$13 a day, the upper line chosen as roughly equivalent to the 2005 US poverty line at 2005 purchasing power parities—in other words, the rising 'bourgeois' were economically equivalent to the American poor. On Ravallion's reckoning, the global middle class had swelled by more than 800 million between 1990 and 2005.

---

[16] In 1990 the World Bank had drawn the 'poverty line' at $375 a year in constant 1985 PPP prices, a threshold later popularized as 'a dollar a day'. Extreme poverty began below $275 a year, corresponding to the official Indian poverty limit: World Bank, *World Development Report 1990*, Oxford 1990, p. 27.

[17] William Easterly, 'The Middle-Class Consensus and Economic Development', World Bank Working Paper no. 2346, May 2000. The term 'middle-class consensus' was thus misleading and should be read as a symptom of the ideological climate of the time. The same article could have been published as 'Equality and Economic Development', which would have framed the problem very differently.

[18] Eric Beinhocker et al., 'Tracking the Growing of India's Middle Class', *McKinsey Quarterly*, no. 3, January 2007; Dominic Wilson and Raluca Dragusanu, 'The Expanding Middle: The Exploding World Middle Class and Falling Global Inequality', Goldman Sachs Global Economic Paper, no. 170, 2008.

A closer look, however, revealed that 622 million of these were in 'developing East Asia', which basically meant China. But if the $2–$13 Chinese middle class had 'exploded' from 15 to 62 per cent of the population, the changes in the other world regions were comparatively modest. In South Asia, those with $2–$13 to spend per day had risen from 17 to 26 per cent of the population; in Africa, from 23 to 26 per cent; in the Middle East and North Africa, from 76 to 79 per cent; in Latin America, from 63 to 66 per cent—though in each case, the new 'bulge' was mainly concentrated at 'just above $2 a day'. Meanwhile in Eastern Europe and Central Asia, the middle class had actually declined slightly, from 76 to 73 per cent.[19]

Seen through this narrow $2–$13 lens, the development of the Asian 'middle class' in the 1990s and 2000s was indeed impressive, eliciting an avalanche of congratulatory literature. The most significant contribution was a 2010 report, 'The Rise of Asia's Middle Class', from the Asian Development Bank, an inter-state body based in Manila. Published in the depths of the recession caused by the 2008 North Atlantic financial crash, the ADB report's press release predicted that 'developing Asia's rapidly expanding middle class is likely to assume the traditional role of the US and Europe as primary global consumers and help rebalance the global economy.' It claimed that Asian consumers would spend 43 per cent of worldwide consumption by 2030.[20] The subtext: the Asian middle class will save the world, or at least the world capitalist economy. According to the ADB, the middle class of 'developing Asia'—that is, excluding Japan—had grown from 569 million to 1.9 billion between 1990 and 2008, or from 21 to 56 per cent of the population. This middle class was now defined as earning $2–$20 a day, the upper limit set at about the poverty line in Italy. The poor, those below $2 a day, had correspondingly shrunk from 79 to 43 per cent. Most of this change was concentrated in China—but not all; the Indian middle class had expanded from 29 to 38 per cent between 1993 and 2005. The figures were based on surveys, and not very robust. Calculations from the national accounts gave a somewhat different picture but with the same impressive tendency, the poor decreasing from 69 to 17 per cent across 'developing Asia', and the 'middle class' rising from 31 to 82 per cent.[21]

[19] Martin Ravallion, 'The Developing World's Bulging (but Vulnerable) "Middle Class"', World Bank Working Paper no. 4816, 2009, Table 3 and p. 17.
[20] Asian Development Bank, 'The Rise of Asia's Middle Class', in *Key Indicators for Asia and the Pacific 2010*, August 2010, part 1.
[21] Asian Development Bank, *Key Indicators for Asia and the Pacific 2010*, Tables 2.1, 2.6 and 2.2.

Fascination with the Asian middle class has not led to any agreement on the actual size of the animal. A Chinese stock-taking some years ago found scholarly estimates of the PRC's middle class that ranged from 4 to 33 per cent, far short of the ADB's boosterish estimate of 89 per cent.[22] The Indian 'middle class' may comprise anything between 10 and 64 per cent of the population. A recent study found that 50 per cent of the population fell within the $2–$10 bracket in 2011–12; interestingly, it puts the 'rise' a decade later than the ADB, not in the 1990s but in the period 2004–12. The lion's share of this was attributable to people moving from less than $2 a day to between $2 and $6 a day.[23] In fact, the most interesting discussion in Asia about the new middle class is probably happening in India, where a heterogeneous intellectual public is debating not just its size and growth but its socio-political meaning, in relation to a national political project of 'changing India'. For Leela Fernandes, it represents 'the political construction of a social group that operates as a proponent of economic liberalization'. For Dipankar Gupta, on the other hand, the term 'middle class' looks 'sickly' in India precisely because there is no project attached to it: instead, 'we are besotted with consumption statistics.'[24]

The question posed by the 2010 ADB report—whether Asia's new middle-class consumers can compensate for falling growth in US middle-class spending power—was also addressed by the World Bank/ Brookings economist Homi Kharas. Using a more intercontinental def-inition of middle-class consumption, $10–$100 a day, Kharas dispensed with descriptions of the class related to democracy, entrepreneurship or 'contributing to human capital and saving'—that is, the entire gamut of traditional middle-class characteristics—insisting instead that 'what makes the middle class special focuses on consumption'. He predicted a rise in the global middle class from 1.8 billion in 2009 to 4.9 bil-lion by 2030, as the world economy pivoted towards Asia, which was expected to account for 85 per cent of the increase, driven primarily by the Indian middle classes (which 'could overtake China by 2020')

[22] Li, The Rising Middle Classes and China, Table 1.
[23] Sandhya Krishnan and Neeraj Hatekar, 'Rise of the New Middle Class in India and Its Changing Structure', Economic and Political Weekly, 2 June 2017, esp. Figure 1a, Table 2. The low ('scheduled') castes experienced an uplift, while the relative advantage of Hindus over Muslims remained about the same (Table 3).
[24] Leela Fernandes, India's New Middle Class, Minneapolis 2006, p. xviii; Dipankar Gupta, The Caged Phoenix: Can India Fly?, New Delhi 2009, p. 83. The uncaring egotism of the middle class is a frequent criticism in India.

and by China.[25] The rise of a huge Asian consumer market is clearly part of an ongoing shift of the global economy. But 'middle class' and 'poverty' are not blank signifiers which can arbitrarily be put to any use. The Tokyo-based economist John West has drawn attention to the distortions created by the conscious or sub-conscious transference of historical Western connotations of 'middle classness' to contemporary Eastern nations, giving rise to what he calls 'Asia's mythical middle-class society'.[26]

African hopes

The African Development Bank followed its Asian counterpart in 2011 with an upbeat report on the *Dynamics of the Middle Class in Africa*: 'the middle class is widely acknowledged to be Africa's future'. Since it was 'associated with better governance, economic growth and poverty reduction', fostering its development 'should be of primary interest to policy makers'.[27] Using the same $2–$10 definition, the report claimed that the African middle class (including North Africa) had increased to 34 per cent of the continent's population by 2010, after stagnating around 28 per cent between 1980 and 2000. At 327 million, it was now 'roughly the size of the middle class in India or China' (a stretch, given that the ADB had claimed a Chinese middle class of 845 million, more than 80 per cent of the total population of Africa in 2010). The ranks of this new African bourgeoisie, as the *Economist* put it, had grown by 122 million since 2000; of these, some 93 million lived on $2–$4 a day. The African Development Bank called this sub tier a 'floating class', vulnerable to slipping back into poverty. Another 23 million, with $4–$10 dollars a day, were members of the 'lower middle class'. Finally, an 'upper middle' at the $10–$20 mark (the lowest rung of Kharas's definition of the global middle class) had actually declined in terms of population share since 1980, falling from 15 to 13 per cent.

Other studies of the African middle class have been more sober. Henning Melber, editor of one of the best collections, notes with bafflement the impact on African studies of the consumptionist approach set out above, initiated by 'a handful of economists'. But Melber also acknowledges

---

[25] Homi Kharas, 'The Emerging Middle Classes in Developing Countries', OECD Development Centre Working Paper 285, 2010, pp. 10–11, 38.
[26] John West, *Asian Century on a Knife-edge*, London 2018.
[27] 'The Middle of the Pyramid: Dynamics of the Middle Class in Africa', AfDB Market Brief, 20 April 2011.

the popular attraction of middle-class identity, drawing on a study of the Black township of Soweto in Johannesburg, where two-thirds of respondents considered themselves middle class in a population where 7 per cent worked in middle-class occupations, 25 per cent were wage workers, 23 per cent were unemployed, 21 per cent were casual labourers and the rest were pensioners or students.[28] By around 2015, the hype about a new African middle class had dissipated. From London, the *Financial Times* reported that foreign corporations were downscaling on the continent for want of middle-class consumers. The *Economist* also took note, now describing the African middle class as 'few and far between'. Both presented starkly reduced estimates of its size: 15 million across eleven of the continent's larger national economies, reported the FT based on a survey by Standard Bank, or just 6 per cent of the population according to the *Economist*, citing the Pew Center.[29]

Latin American circumspection

Latin American interest in the middle class also intensified in 2010, but took a very different form. The hype was absent, and socio-economic and sociological perspectives were more prominent than $2 head counts. The lower level of excitement had its background in the hemisphere's undistinguished ranking in middle-class growth tables: a rise of just 3 percentage points between 1990 and 2005 according to Ravallion, as cited above. From 2010, three major reports appeared. *The Middle Class in Latin America*, a sociological analysis combining an occupational class approach and income distribution, was published by CEPAL, the UN Economic Commission for Latin America—a rough equivalent of the Asian Development Bank and an important actor in analytical and policy discussions in the region. Meanwhile a socio-economic assessment came from the Americas desk of the OECD Development Centre in its annual *Latin American Economic Outlook 2011*, subtitled 'How Middle Class is Latin America?'. Three years later the World Bank put out a weighty contribution, *Economic Mobility and the Rise of the Latin*

---

[28] Henning Melber, '"Somewhere above Poor but below Rich": Explorations into the Species of the African Middle Class(es)', in Melber, ed., *The Rise of Africa's Middle Class*, London 2016, p. 3. Another noteworthy overview-cum-contribution is James Thurlow, Danielle Resnick and Dumebi Ubogu, 'Matching Concepts with Measurement: Who Belongs to Africa's Middle Class?', *Journal of International Development*, vol. 27, no. 5, July 2015.
[29] 'Nestlé Cuts Africa Workforce as Middle-Class Growth Disappoints', *Financial Times*, 17 June 2015; 'Few and Far Between', *Economist*, 24 October 2015.

American Middle Class. These institutional responses used different class definitions and painted three different pictures of Latin America.

The CEPAL study proceeded from the question, 'What are we talking about when we talk about the middle class?', and drew a map of social stratification in which the 'middle strata'—the term used in preference to 'middle class'—could be located. The middle strata were defined in terms of occupation (white collar) and income (four times the urban poverty line). While the study identified a substantial growth in the size of these social layers, overwhelmingly due to an increase of the lower middle, its conclusions emphasized social heterogeneity and inter-country variation, illustrated by five concluding monographs on contrasted countries.[30]

The contribution from the OECD Development Centre was policy oriented and aimed to identify the conditions of middle-class support. The guiding assumption was that if these sectors had 'stable employment and reasonably robust incomes', they would provide 'a solid foundation for economic progress', while if they had 'precarious incomes and unstable employment', then 'their political preferences may veer toward populist platforms not necessarily conducive to good economic management.'[31] These 'middle sectors' were defined by their very middleness: that is, households with an income of 50–150 per cent of median income, an unmotivated expansion of the more common 75–125 per cent range once proposed by the distinguished economist Lester Thurow. The effect was inflationary: the OECD's 'middle sectors' contained more contract-less 'informal' workers than formal employees.[32] The report also provided a comparison of Italian and Latin American trends. While the 'middle sectors' comprise over 60 per cent of Italy's population, in Uruguay and Mexico they make up about 50 per cent, in Chile and Brazil around 45 per cent, in Argentina 40 per cent, and in Colombia and Bolivia just over a third. With regard to policy prospects, the OECD report ends on a cautiously optimistic note about the middle sectors and the potential for positive changes in income distribution, social protection and opportunity creation.

---

[30] Arturo León, et al., 'Clases medias en América Latina: Una visión de sus cambios en las últimas dos décadas', in Rolando Franco, Martín Hopenhayn and Arturo León, eds, *La clase media en América Latina*, Mexico City and Buenos Aires 2010, pp. 95ff.
[31] OECD, *Latin American Economic Outlook 2011: How Middle-Class Is Latin America?*, 3 December 2010, p. 15.
[32] OECD, *Latin American Economic Outlook 2011*, p. 62.

The World Bank product on Latin America was an elaborate investigation with two main themes, income mobility and the rising volume of the middle class. It starts with a fanfare: the continent is 'a middle-income region on the way to becoming a middle-class region'. But the music becomes more subdued along the way: the region is not yet a 'middle-class society' where 'most people earn a sufficiently high income to consume, live and behave [sic] like middle-class citizens'. In fact, 'vulnerability to poverty remains a serious concern for the majority, and social policies will continue to play an important role for the foreseeable future.' Nevertheless, the World Bank predicts a great future for the Latin American middle class: by 2030 it will have grown from a mere 30 per cent to a convincing 40 per cent of the continent's population.[33]

Drawing on the 'vulnerability approach' proposed by two World Bank colleagues,[34] the report launched yet another definition of the 'middle class', now based on economic security—once again ignoring the historical connotations of the term. On this basis, the middle class are those with a less than 10 per cent probability of falling into poverty within five years. In some Latin American countries this would translate into a household per capita income of $10 a day; in others, it would not. The authors pragmatically settle for $10 a day as their lower bound. Without providing any substantiating rationale, they also add an upper bound of $50 a day. On this basis, they declared that the Latin American middle class had doubled between 1992 and 2009, rising from 15.5 per cent of the population to nearly 30 per cent.[35]

In sum, the highest-flying Southern middle-class dreams have been Asian, concentrated in China and India, although they have encompassed all of 'developing Asia' apart from the western war zones. In this twenty-first-century imaginary, the Global South is surfing an ever-rising middle-class wave, the most important social change of the age. At its most far-reaching, the middle-class dream was linked to a shift in the centre of global economic gravity, from North America and Europe to Asia. If there was no consensus on the shape and content of this class,

[33] Francisco H. G. Ferreira, et al., *Economic Mobility and the Rise of the Latin American Middle Class*, World Bank, 2013, pp. 136, 144ff.
[34] Luis F. López-Calva and Eduardo Ortiz-Juarez, 'A Vulnerability Approach to the Definition of the Middle Class', World Bank Working Paper 5902, December 2011.
[35] Ferreira et al., *Economic Mobility and the Rise of the Latin American Middle Class*, pp. 32–6, 147.

nor on the pace of its growth, it was widely agreed that it would mean more money and more consumption. The future understandably looks more modest viewed from Abidjan or Santiago de Chile, the headquarters of the African Development Bank and CEPAL respectively. In both Africa and Latin America, the middle-class dream has more often had some contact with the realities of social structure. But the Southern dream persists; the latest prediction from Homi Kharas suggests that by 2030 the 'middle class' will be dominant, with 63 per cent of the world's population.[36]

2. NORTHERN NIGHTMARES

While the middle classes were touted as 'rising', 'expanding' and 'exploding' in the South, they were found to be shrinking in the North. 'We have observed', concluded leading inequality scholars Anthony Atkinson and Andrea Brandolini, 'a downsizing of the middle class from the mid-1980s to the mid-2000s'. In a study of fifteen OECD countries, the 'middle 60 per cent' lost income shares 'to the benefit of the richest fifth' in all except Denmark, and in ten countries the middle class actually shrank.[37] In 2011, Francis Fukuyama wondered aloud: 'But what if the further development of technology and globalization undermines the middle class and makes it impossible for more than a minority of citizens in an advanced society to achieve middle-class status?' Indeed, 'there are already abundant signs that such a phase of development has begun.' Fukuyama then raised an even bigger fear: 'Can liberal democracy survive the decline of the middle class?'[38]

The OECD has been worried about increasing inequality in the rich countries since its 2008 *Growing Unequal?* report, but it took a further decade before it focused on the difficulties of the middle class. In

---

[36] Kharas, 'Global Tipping Point'. I have not seen any new middle-class stories by him since the start of the pandemic.
[37] Anthony Atkinson and Andrea Brandolini, 'On the Identification of the Middle Class', in Janet Gornick and Markus Jäntti, eds, *Income Inequality: Economic Disparities and the Middle Class in Affluent Countries*, Stanford CA 2013, p. 95. In the context of this shrinking, the middle class is defined by intervals around national median income (75–125 per cent of the median) and also by other, wider intervals: p. 85.
[38] Francis Fukuyama, 'The Future of History: Can Liberal Democracy Survive the Decline of the Middle Class?', *Foreign Affairs*, Jan–Feb 2012, p. 7.

2018 it put out an overview of darkening middle-class views on social mobility, socio-economic status in comparison with their parents, and future prospects.[39] There followed in 2019 a wider-ranging study, *Under Pressure: The Squeezed Middle Class*—no question mark added—using a band of 75–200 per cent of median disposable income as its definition of the middle class. The size of this population in OECD—i.e., rich-world—countries shrank on average from 64 to 61 per cent between the mid-1980s and the mid-2010s. Its distance from the rich has widened, the income of the wealthiest 10 per cent increasing by a third more than that of the middle class. In addition, middle-class income share has fallen more than its population share, dropping 5 percentage points; the upshot has been rising debt—20 per cent of middle-class households now spend more than they earn. Sweden is outstanding in squeezing its middle class: population share has fallen by 7 percentage points, income share by 11 points. The corresponding figures for the US are 4 and 9 points; the British middle class has stayed put as a proportion of the population while losing 5 points of its income share.[40]

The only positive development in the North has been the increased entry of the over-65s into the ranks of the middle-income class, except in the US. For the rest, *Under Pressure* paints a grim picture, concluding that 'many middle-class households consider our socio-economic system unfair' because they haven't benefited from it as much as high-income groups. Furthermore, a 'middle-class lifestyle is increasingly expensive, notably when it comes to housing, a good education and health care'. Labour-market prospects for many in the middle class are uncertain: one in six middle-income workers are in jobs 'at high risk of automation'. *Under Pressure* is not apocalyptic, in contrast to the stream of national lamentations we shall look at below, but it tersely comments that, for many, 'the middle-class dream is increasingly only a dream'.[41] What has gone wrong?

The Northern middle-class downturn started in the US in the late 1970s. It was brought to public notice through the work of a few sharp-eyed observers in the course of the mid-80s, though their findings were at first denied by mainstream opinion leaders. In 1986 a Federal Reserve economist, Katherine Bradbury, published a paper on 'The Shrinking Middle Class', which found a decline of 5 percentage points

---

[39] OECD, *A Broken Social Elevator? How to Promote Social Mobility*, 15 June 2018.
[40] OECD, *Under Pressure: The Squeezed Middle Class*, 1 May 2019, pp. 13, 50.
[41] OECD, *Under Pressure*, pp. 32, 16, Table 2.2.

in the proportion of families with incomes of $20,000–$50,000 during 1973–84, of which 4 points were due to downward mobility.[42] In their excellent book, *The Great U-Turn*, Bennett Harrison and Barry Bluestone situated this fall in the context of historical developments within American capitalism: falling profits due to foreign competition leading to deindustrialization, corporate restructuring and financialization, hollowing out and polarizing the US labour market. 'Does all this portend an end to the middle class in America?', the authors asked. But these were pre-apocalyptic times, and they replied in the negative: 'the middle class in America is resilient. Workers struggle to maintain their wages against the force of deindustrialization'.[43]

Following the crash of 2008, even the official tone darkened. A White House task force set up by the Obama Administration to study the problem used bland and cautious language, defining 'middle class' with an ideological emphasis on 'aspirations'—to home ownership; college education for their children; health and retirement security; family vacations. The principal finding was that, with the cost of health care, college and housing rising faster than incomes, it had become 'more difficult' now for many Americans 'to achieve middle-class status'.[44] As the decade progressed, the tone became more apocalyptic. In 2017, MIT economist Peter Temin marshalled evidence to show that the American middle class—now defined as those with 67–200 per cent of US median income—was vanishing; its income share had dropped from 63 per cent in 1970 to 43 per cent in 2014. This hollowing middle was leaving the US a 'dual economy', in the sense of Arthur Lewis's analysis of Third World capitalism, with an FTE sector (finance, technology, electronics) comprising about 20 per cent of the population and setting the rules for the economy, while a low-wage sector harboured the remaining 80 per cent.[45]

---

[42] Katherine Bradbury, 'The Shrinking Middle Class', *New England Economic Review*, Sept–Oct 1986.

[43] Bennett Harrison and Barry Bluestone, *The Great U-Turn*, New York 1988, p. 137; Note that in contemporary US idiom, industrial workers are often included in the 'middle class'. Cf. William Kreml, *America's Middle Class: From Subsidy to Abandonment*, Durham NC 1997.

[44] Office of the Vice President, Middle Class Task Force, 'Middle Class in America', January 2010.

[45] Temin, *Vanishing Middle Class*. Daniel Markovits, a law scholar at Yale, highlights the hoarding of increasingly costly top education by a rich elite, from pre-school to university, and how this kind of meritocracy has 'banished the majority of citizens to the margins of their own society, consigning middle-class children to lacklustre schools and dead-end jobs': *The Meritocracy Trap*, London 2019, pp. xiii–xiv.

The implications of capitalism's new turn for the European middle classes were discovered relatively late.[46] Only in the past decade have middle-class nightmares come to haunt European writers, following the financial crash of 2008. In the UK, the director of a 'radical centre' think-tank anguished in *Broke: Who Killed the Middle Classes?* about their 'impoverishment' and 'corrosion', warning that 'the destruction wreaked on the working classes is now in store for them'—and wondering if Marx would belatedly be proved right: capitalism might yet culminate in the proletarianization of the middle classes. In Germany, journalist Daniel Goffart announced 'the end of the middle stratum'—here, those on 70–150 per cent of median income—which had declined from 48 to 41 per cent of the population between 1991 and 2015, with a further threat to employment looming from digitalization. In France, the social geographer Christophe Guilluy announced 'the end of the Western middle class', a concept which for him was 'above all cultural', its disappearance measured 'by the loss of a status' embodying the European or American way of life; the 'popular categories, workers and employees' had now been downgraded 'from desirables to deplorables'.[47]

3. THE MIDDLE CLASSES BY DAYLIGHT

In this brief survey of the recent literature we have met a bewildering variety of groupings labelled 'middle class'. Clearly, as Ferreira and his World Bank colleagues observe in their study of Latin America, 'defining the middle class is no trivial matter'.[48] While definitions as such are neither correct nor incorrect, they may be illuminating or obfuscating, in line with historical usage or arbitrarily idiosyncratic; when clothed in everyday language, novel definitions may have misleading connotations. In other words, the concepts underlying these dreams and nightmares need to be scrutinized by daylight. The Southern middle-class dreamworld is

---

[46] In 2002, a major Euro-centred overview of 'the middle classes of America, Europe and Japan' focused not on crisis or decline, but on the 'stress' placed on post-war social contracts by economic globalization; the findings of Harrison and Bluestone were not even mentioned. Although the appearance of 'middle-class angst' in the late 1990s is noted by one of the editors, only Japan is seen to be in crisis mode, in an obituary by Harvard Japanologist Andrew Gordon of 'The Short Happy Life of the Japanese Middle Class' in the post-war period. See Olivier Zunz, Leonard Schoppa and Nobuhiro Hiwatari, eds, *Social Contracts under Stress*, New York 2002.
[47] Respectively: David Boyle, *Broke: Who Killed the Middle Classes?*, London 2013, pp. 315, 273; Daniel Goffart, *Das Ende der Mittelschicht*, Munich 2019, p. 36; Christophe Guilluy, *No society: La fin de la classe moyenne occidentale*, Paris 2018, pp. 77–9.
[48] Ferreira et al., *Economic Mobility and the Rise of the Latin American Middle Class*, p. 1.

premised on a zero-sum linkage between the middle class and poverty; the rise of one is the flipside of the other's decline. As we have noted, this is literally a bankers' and business consultants' outlook—Goldman Sachs, McKinsey, the corporate-oriented development banks, the World Bank—and it frames the world in a very peculiar way: wide-angled at times, it is only capable of seeing a world of trade and consumption; there are no producers, no working class and no social relations.

In bankers' eyes, 'middle class' and 'poverty' are defined solely by the dollar sign. The relational and the relative have been absolutized and turned in upon themselves. *Middle* class is an intrinsically relative concept, denoting a stratum between at least two others. Poverty refers to having fewer resources in relation to relevant others, as indicated by the fact that rich and poor countries draw different poverty lines. In this sense, poverty is also relative. This discourse has an incentive, economic and political, to drain these terms of sociological meaning, as this allows one to be inflated and the other diminished. Yet using an everyday-language concept like 'middle class' with an idiosyncratic technical definition can mislead the reader, and to treat such a historically established and socio-politically charged concept in this way is either unwise or dishonest. The frequent counts of the Southern 'middle class'—or, more cautiously, 'middle sectors'—as those on $2–$4 a day include street vendors, day labourers and other contract-less and rights-less workers. Sixty per cent of the OECD's Latin American 'middle sectors' are in the informal economy.[49] It apparently requires an exceptional mind to discern workers in the middle-class haze of the Southern dreamworld.

In 2008, a study by Abhijit Banerjee and Esther Duflo posed the question, 'What is middle class about the world's middle classes?' Looking at households with a per capita expenditure of $2–$10 and drawing on extensive Third World research, they found that 'while there are many petty entrepreneurs among the middle class, most of them do not seem to be capitalists in waiting. They run businesses, but for the most part only because they are still relatively poor and every little bit helps.' Why is this important? 'It leads us to the idea of a "good job"'—an idea that economists have often resisted, 'on the grounds that good jobs may be expensive jobs.' But, Banerjee and Duflo conclude, 'nothing seems more middle class than the fact of having a steady well-paying job'.[50]

---

[49] 'Latin American Economic Outlook 2011', p. 89.
[50] Abhijit Banerjee and Esther Duflo, 'What is Middle Class about the Middle Classes around the World?', *Journal of Economic Perspectives*, vol. 22, no. 2, 2008.

The logic of the Southern dreamworld suggests that the expansion of the 'middle classes' means that poverty is about to disappear, just as it supposedly has in large parts of the North. According to the World Bank, poverty in Europe—measured as less than \$3.20 a day—is non-existent: at this level, the poverty rate stands at zero in France, Germany and the UK; in Sweden, it is a mere 1 per cent. By contrast, looking at broader indicators, the Eurostat economists more convincingly see 22 per cent of the EU population 'at risk of poverty and social exclusion'.[51] For poverty is a social concept, not a biological one, nor a quantity of money below a certain line. As such it is intrinsically relational, referring to a disposal of resources below the median, regardless of whether it is defined as 'absolute'—below some monetary level—or as 'relative', below some percentage of the population.

If the Southern rise of the middle class looks less rosy in the clear light of day, its Northern apocalypse looks less calamitous. Since the mid-8os, the OECD middle classes—defined at 75–200 per cent of median income—have on average declined from 64 to 61 per cent of the population, while their share of national income has decreased by 5 percentage points. Sweden and the US were the epicentres of decline, with middle-class income shares falling by 11 and 9 percentage points, respectively—although despite this, it's interesting that Sweden has not yet been a subject for 'middle-class nightmare' discourse. In France, Ireland and Denmark, on the other hand, the economic middle has (slightly) increased in size over this period.[52] The problems encountered by Northern youth and young adults in accessing higher education and accommodation are real enough, in rich-world countries with high university fees and marketized housing. But the literature concentrating on the middle class fails to see the systematic inequalities produced by contemporary post-industrial capitalism. Its discourse is the nightmare of a class attempting to isolate itself from these dynamics. But in what directions do they tend?

4. CONVERGING ROADS TO INEQUALITY

To paraphrase Oscar Wilde on England and America, we may say that the Global South and the Global North are divided by a common class.

---

[51] Eurostat, 'Europe 2020 Indicators—Poverty and Social Exclusion', August 2019.
[52] OECD, *Under Pressure*, p. 19 and Figure 2.5.

However, the evidence suggests these 'middle classes' are converging on the highway of twenty-first-century capitalist inequality. The Southerners are coming from poverty and the Northerners from relative comfort, but it seems likely that they are going to find each other, struggling and striving, abandoned by an ever-richer bourgeoisie, and with uncertain relations to the popular classes of workers, precariat and unemployed. And though they are nationally divided, they live under the same climate cloud (and face similar viral risks). Certain trends are apparent, even if we restrict our examination to income share.

Since the upper limit for the Southern middle class in Ravallion's World Bank overview was the US poverty line, the recent trajectory and social horizons of the US poor may well indicate something about the future of the 'rising' Southern middle classes. The poorest Americans, around 20 per cent of the US population, are roughly equivalent to the Southern 'middle classes'.[53] As Table 1 shows, their experience since 1980 has been of falling further behind. What Thomas Piketty's team at the World Inequality Lab call the 'middle forty per cent'—the core and upper ranks of the American middle class—have also lost ground to the rich, or what may properly be called the bourgeoisie. The US development is extreme, but not *sui generis*. Between 1985 and 2017, the British 'middle forty' lost 4 percentage points of its income share, while the top ten increased its

TABLE 1: *Growth of Income in the US, 1980–2014, per cent*

Full adult population	41
Bottom 20%	4
Next 30%	26
Bottom 50%	21
Middle 40%	49
Top 10%	113
Top 1%	194

Figures are after taxes and transfers. Source: Facundo Alvaredo et al.,
World Inequality Report 2018, World Inequality Lab, 2017, Table 2.4.2.

[53] Americans with incomes up to 125 per cent of the national poverty line (currently $26,200 p/a for a household of four) make up some 20 per cent of the US population.

share by 5 points. In Germany, the top ten appropriated 8 extra percentage points of national income, while the 'middle' lost 1 point, and in France the 'middle' lost 2 points and the top ten gained 3 points.[54]

The Northern experience, then, suggests that the next stage up from poverty is the experience of widening inequality, which for those at the losing end represents another kind of poverty—the consciousness of having only meagre resources with which to get by in life—tacitly recognized as such by the ruling authorities of the North. Will the Southern middle classes meet a similar fate? It's worth recalling that the Global North experienced a period of 'inclusive growth'—that is, growth with decreasing inequality—in the 1945–80 period, the time of labour-movement influence. The Southern middle-class dreamers are deliberately erasing the memory of those times, but the question should be asked: is any equalization in sight in the South? A thorough answer would require another essay. As Table 2 shows, however, ongoing distributive tendencies in China and India point to a non-lagged convergence on the road of mounting inequality. In other words, yesterday's Southern dreams are likely to turn into nightmares similar to those of the North.

In China and India, heartlands of the 'rising middle class', even the 'middle forty' is losing ground: the income growth rate for the bottom 50 per cent of the population is less than half that of the whole population. In India growth for the 'middle forty' has been just half of the national average. Neoliberal India has become the US of the Global South—and, like the US, has a clear historical U-curve of economic inequality. The

TABLE 2: *Pre-Tax Income Growth as Percent of National Growth, 1980–2015*

	China	India	USA	France
Bottom 50%	47	48	2	71
Middle 40%	93	50	69	91
Top 10%	163	211	198	134
Top 1%	233	401	334	251

Source: Calculations from Alvaredo et al. *World Inequality Report 2018*, Table 2.9.1

[54] World Inequality Database, national tables.

income share of the Indian top one per cent is back to its level in the colonial 1930s.[55] The virtual exclusion of the bottom half of the US population from sharing the proceeds of economic growth over the past thirty years tells us something important about capitalist democracy.

The probable future in store for the Southern middle classes under the current world system is highlighted in Table 3.[56] It should be kept in mind that the Northern figures refer to disposable income after taxes and transfers: in other words, they include the remaining, if eroded, effects of the 1945–80 equalization, a period such as the South has not yet entered, and which under present conditions perhaps never will.

Developments in China and India are crucial, but they cannot be assumed to hold for the whole of the South. Empirical data are still lacking for many big countries in Asia and Africa, but the figures that do exist indicate some diversity. In Brazil, under the PT governments, the income of the bottom half of the population grew faster than that of the nation; but in absolute terms, the top 10 per cent captured 58 per cent of total income growth, and the bottom half, 16 per cent.[57] Inequality has been rampant in post-apartheid South Africa, with the bottom half and the upper-middle class (the 50th to 90th percentiles) each losing about 10 percentage points of national income share, to the benefit of the top decile. In Nigeria, the bottom 90 per cent are also losing out heavily to the richest 10 per cent. In Turkey, Thailand and Malaysia, on the other

---

TABLE 3: *Northern Upper Class: Income Ratios of the Top 1% to the Median*

Germany (post-tax)	*1990*	7.2	*2016*	11.5
Sweden (disposable income)	*1991*	3.5	*2016*	10.7
UK (household net income)	*1980*	3.3	*2018*	9.9
US (post-tax income)	*1980*	11.2	*2014*	25.8

France is an exception, going from a ratio of 10.5 to 9.6 between 1990 and 2014. Sources: Statistics Sweden, Institute for Fiscal Studies (London) and World Inequality Database.

---

[55] Facundo Alvaredo, et al., *World Inequality Report 2018*, World Inequality Lab, 2017, pp. 127ff.
[56] Median incomes in the South are not included in the World Inequality Database.
[57] Alvaredo, et al., *World Inequality Report 2018*, Table 2.11.3.

hand, some economic equalization has occurred. Egyptian income distribution has changed less over the past three decades, according to the World Inequality Database, but there has been a growing concentration of income at the top.[58]

Most important for future trends: nowhere in the South is there any evidence of a sustained egalitarian drive. There was such a tendency in Latin America in the first decade of the century, but it has been halted—by right-wing politics, above all, but also recently in Mexico by COVID-19.[59] New rounds in the battle between equality and privilege lie around the corner, in Argentina and Chile. But for now, growing inequality remains the most likely outcome.

5. A POLITICAL OUTLOOK

Those who hope that the rising middle classes will bring about a good society—given what the OECD calls 'their intolerance of corruption, and their trust in others'—need to take account of the ambitious young Modi supporters described by Snigdha Poonam in *Dreamers*: the middle-class aspirants who run sophisticated online and call-centre scams from small-town India, churning out clickbait, selling fake jobs and diplomas or extorting money from elderly Americans by threatening them with the Internal Revenue Service.[60]

The middle-class discourses should rather be read symptomatically, as an expression of larger processes of development. In the North, the key point is that the prevailing middle-class literature is essentially a critique, though often oblique, of the ongoing increase of inequality. It is not a narrative of a middle class threatened from below by trade unions or state handouts to the poor. It is about a class being abandoned, left behind by a previously admired economic leadership and lifestyle model. In other words, it is an objectively progressive discourse, despite its occasional apocalyptic self-pity. It may indicate a sizeable potential

[58] World Inequality Database.
[59] CEPAL put out a report titled *La hora de igualdad* [The Hour of Equality], Santiago 2010. See also my own attempt at analysis, 'Moments of Equality: Today's Latin America in a Global Context', in Barbara Fritz and Lena Lavinas, eds, *A Moment of Equality for Latin America*, Farnham 2015.
[60] Snigdha Poonam, *Dreamers*, Cambridge MA, 2018; see also OECD, *Under Pressure*, p. 13.

base for progressive taxation. As the OECD's *Under Pressure* shows, the 'squeeze' on the Northern middle class mainly affects the young and young middle-age generation born after 1975–80.[61] This was the generation that rallied behind the surprisingly successful campaigns of Corbyn and Sanders.

The field of work is another meeting-ground for the left, the labour movement and the salaried middle class. There is a growing contradiction between, on the one hand, the middle-class professionalism of teachers, health personnel, public-service employees and civil servants, and on the other, the increasingly invasive capitalist-managerial notion of labour for profit. The latter is, and should be, an affront to every true professional, who takes pride in learnt expertise and pleasure in the intrinsic value of her work. The incipient digital revolution is likely to hit the professions hard, as well as the mass of white-collar employees. A widespread middle-class environmentalism is already clashing with the accumulation drive of real-estate developers, ruthless extraction corporations and producers of pollution. The Southern growth of the 'middle class', however defined, is part of a rapid, large-scale social change which will never create an industry-centred—and thereby a socio-politically industrial working-class centred—society similar to that previously found in the North. Industrial and manufacturing employment has already started to decline in Asia and Latin America, and is most unlikely to grow beyond current Asian levels in Africa.[62] The social structuring of forces for equality and social justice will be different this time around.

It is already clear that the COVID-19 pandemic is a Great Unequalizer, virally as well as economically, with ferocious discrimination within as well as between classes, between men and women, generations and ethnic groups. What this means for the dreams and nightmares we have been examining is an accelerated convergence of the Northern and the Southern middle classes on the bleak path of inequality. Their common abandonment by big digital capital, headed by Amazon and Microsoft,

---

[61] OECD, *Under Pressure*, pp. 55, 57. Despite the lamentations of Guilluy and others, the French middle class has maintained itself economically better than in many other rich countries, but the generational prospects for people born after 1975 have followed the OECD mainstream downward: Louis Chauvel, *Les classes moyennes à la dérive*, Paris 2006.

[62] *Trade and Development Report 2016*, United Nations Conference on Trade and Development, 21 September 2016; Dani Rodrik, 'Premature Deindustrialisation', NBER Working Paper 20935, February 2015; 'Employment in Industry', ILOSTAT, 2019.

has been magnified many times over. Most of the Northern middle class of small business and freelance 'entrepreneurs' have been economic losers in the Coronavirus crisis. Even more so are the Southern informal workers on $2–$6 dollars a day, supposedly incorporated into the middle-class conglomerate, but now likely to fall back into raw poverty. The World Bank and CEPAL have already signalled that the much-touted decline of extreme poverty in the world will be reversed.[63] By contrast, in North and South alike, upper middle-class managers, bureaucrats and professionals have had a relatively good crisis, keeping their salaries and safely working from home.

The 2020 pandemic has therefore divided the middle class, while the gap between its upper ranks and the real bourgeoisie is widening further, due to the billions of dollars of pandemic 'stimulus' snaffled by the latter.[64] Middle-class aspirations are being thwarted by a surge in youth unemployment, in both North and South. The 'forward march' of the Southern middle class, by whatever definition, has halted. Northern nightmares, on the other hand, are likely to continue. The frenetic preoccupation with consumption in mainstream middle-class discourse might appear frivolous in the shadow of the Coronavirus, and under the darkening clouds of climate change.

Further important questions—the processes of contemporary middle-class formation, social development and political potential—lie beyond the scope of this paper. For now, what conclusions may be drawn? First, the world can only be understood through its differences and inequalities, taking a 360-degree perspective. Failing that, the world looks very different depending on one's vantage point; a vista from the North may look upside down from the South, and vice versa. Second, the middle class has a discursive centrality in the early twenty-first century, corresponding to that of the working class a century before. It should be

---

[63] Carolina Sánchez-Páramo, 'COVID-19 Will Hit the Poor Hardest. Here's What We Can Do About It', World Bank Voices Blog, 23 April 2020; Alicia Bárcena, 'El desafío social en tiempos de COVID-19', CEPAL, 12 May 2020. The UNDP is calling COVID-19 a 'systemic crisis in human development': 'COVID-19 and Human Development: Assessing the Crisis, Envisioning the Recovery', UNDP, 20 May 2020, p. 5.
[64] See Robert Brenner, 'Escalating Plunder', NLR 123, May–June 2020. See also 'Prospering in the Pandemic', Financial Times, 18 June 2020. Jeff Bezos had personally gained $34.5 billion by 4 June.

read symptomatically, as an indicator of profound social change, as well as critically, as an ideology of consumer capitalism. Third, prevailing middle-class discourse is deeply—if not always deliberately—ideological, inflating out of all proportion a nebulous entity with strong political connotations—the middle class—and portraying a world of consumers without producers. Fourth, this discourse is also deceptive in absolutizing both the middle class and poverty. Poverty is always relative, the losing end of the prevailing level of unequal resource distribution; and the middle has to be in the middle of something. Finally, the emergent middle classes of the South are heading into the maelstrom of capitalist inequality, where they look set to converge with the hard-hit middle classes of the North. The COVID-19 pandemic is currently shattering the middle-class dream in the South and accelerating the inegalitarian tendencies analysed above. Where this will lead is still an open question.

NEW FROM UNC PRESS

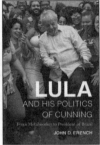

LULA AND HIS POLITICS OF CUNNING
From Metalworker to President of Brazil
John D. French
"This impressive biography of Lula, drawing on French's unparalleled knowledge of modern Brazilian history, benefits from French's thoughtful meditations on the possibilities and limits of leadership; his attention to language and meaning, which can't be reduced to class but rather can construct class identity; and his analysis of how a 'cunning' leader can create unity from divergence."
—**Greg Grandin**, author of the Pulitzer Prize-winning *The End of the Myth*
512 pages $29.95

FROM HERE TO EQUALITY
Reparations for Black Americans in the Twenty-First Century
William A. Darity Jr. and A. Kirsten Mullen
"An extraordinary accomplishment and a brilliant and provocative contribution to the current debate on reparations. Provides a genuinely novel and thoughtful solution that will propel this evolving, international political movement."
—**Craig Steven Wilder**, author of *Ebony and Ivy*
416 pages $28.00

Finalist for the Pulitzer Prize and National Book Award —
RACE FOR PROFIT
How Banks and the Real Estate Industry Undermined Black Homeownership
Keeanga-Yamahtta Taylor
"Details bungling mismanagement, gross corruption, distorted incentives, civil rights regulations that went unheeded and unenforced — what Taylor calls a system of "predatory inclusion" that was distinct yet not entirely free from the racist system of exclusion that preceded it."
—*The New York Times*
368 pages $30.00

AN ANTHROPOLOGY OF MARXISM
Cedric J. Robinson
Second Edition
Preface by Avery F. Gordon, with a new foreword by H. L. T. Quan
"Cedric Robinson was a great and wonderful man and a brilliant scholar. Everything he wrote is of incalculable value, and this book is no exception. Both because of the revolutionary importance of its thesis and because of its erudition and elegance, this book remains indispensable."
—**Fred Moten**, New York University
204 pages $29.95 paper

UNC PRESS **THE UNIVERSITY *of* NORTH CAROLINA PRESS**
at bookstores or 800-848-6224 · uncpress.org · uncpressblog.com

GAVIN RAE

IN THE POLISH MIRROR

THE VICTORY OF the incumbent, Andrzej Duda, in Poland's presidential poll on 12 July 2020 confirms the continuing electoral hold of the conservative-nationalist Law and Justice Party (PiS). 'A blow to liberal hopes', announced the *Economist*, as Duda saw off his challenger, the Civic Platform (PO)'s Rafał Trzaskowski, a neoliberal 'modernizer' and currently mayor of Warsaw, by 51 to 49 per cent in the second round.[1] The *Economist*'s hope had been that a PO president would be able to veto PiS legislation; but despite a historically high turnout of 68 per cent, the West's preferred party was still too tarnished and the hegemony of the PiS, backed by the public broadcaster TVP, too strong. Indeed, since the PiS landslide in 2015, followed by its further win in the 2019 parliamentary elections, Western liberals observing the country give the impression of staring into a distorting mirror: reflected back at them is a dystopian vision of the capitalist democracy they once laboured to create. These Cold War veterans had romanticized the Polish case, adopting Solidarność's symbols as their own. Freed from the Communist yoke, the country would emerge as a beacon of economic liberalism, political democracy and Church-led social stability. Nowadays, Poland's former friends look on in despair, searching for answers as to what has gone wrong.

Two of Poland's closest intellectual allies, the *Guardian's* Timothy Garton Ash and Anne Applebaum of the *Atlantic*, may serve as examples. In 2011, Garton Ash had congratulated the country for 'getting to grips with being normal at last' under the pro-business Civic Platform government of Donald Tusk. A few years later, after Civic Platform had gone down to ignominious defeat in the 2015 elections amid a welter of corruption allegations, while Tusk was helicopered off to head the European Council, Garton Ash declared himself shocked to see 'how far the pillars of liberal, pluralist democracy in Poland have been battered and shaken.'

Resorting, apophatically, to the hoariest central-European stereotypes, he now chastized the 2017 pro-choice demonstrators: 'I won't go so far as the old quip that the Germans can make any system work and the Poles can destroy any system, but certainly we see a contrast between a German strength in making the state work and the Polish forte of society organizing itself against the state.' The noxious populists of PiS were infiltrating their people into the offices of state. Only a countervailing infusion of young Polish liberals into state institutions could 'strengthen the immune system of a still alarmingly fragile democracy.'[2]

Likewise, Applebaum mourns the 'heady optimism' of the early millennium when she and her high-flying husband, Radosław Sikorski, thought as one with their elite circles of Polish and Atlanticist friends. She recalls a 1999 New Year's Eve party at their 'small manor house' between Poznan and Gdańsk, with journalists, diplomats, government ministers, 'friends who flew over from New York'—anti-Communists, conservatives, classical liberals, free-market liberals, Thatcherites. 'It felt as if we were all on the same team', believing in 'a Poland that was a member of NATO and on its way to joining the European Union'; that was what 'being on the right' meant. Today, the Polish right is deeply divided and Applebaum is no longer on speaking terms with half her guests, now backers of the 'nativist', 'xenophobic', 'paranoid', 'authoritarian' PiS, its discourse equally hostile towards Germany, Russia and the EU. What has caused the transformation? Like Garton Ash, Applebaum avoids any element of self-criticism—her husband resigned in disgrace as Polish Foreign Minister during the 2014 'Waitergate' scandal at a swanky Warsaw restaurant, when he and the Interior Minister were caught comparing US–Polish relations to oral sex, over a $500 dinner of baby lobsters and Cuban cigars, on the taxpayer's złoty; Sikorski still stands as a symbol of the corrupt and out-of-touch PO elite. Instead, Applebaum's *Twilight of Democracy* offers weightless musings on the authoritarian personality, the *trahison des clercs*, the genealogy of one-party systems and decline into cultural conservatism of the Polish Church, once 'an apolitical symbol of national unity'.[3]

---

[1] 'A nasty election', *Economist*, 18 July 2020.
[2] Garton Ash, 'Poland: A Country Getting to Grips with Being Normal at Last', *Guardian*, 4 April 2011; 'As Well as Protesting, Poles Need to Strengthen Their State', *Guardian*, 5 January 2017. Poland's 2020 presidential election once again saw 'the future of its democracy' at stake: Garton Ash, 'For a Bitter Taste of Polish Populism, Just Watch the Evening News', *Guardian*, 25 June 2020.
[3] Applebaum, *Twilight of Democracy*, New York 2020, pp. 1–7.

Poland's liberal friends warn that a groundswell of authoritarian populism has arisen in the East, consolidating power in Budapest and
Warsaw. Liberal thinkers in Poland propound similar ideas. Sławomir
Sierakowski of the Institute for Advanced Study in Warsaw argues that
authoritarianism is both stronger and different in Central and Eastern
Europe, due to a lack of post-materialist values and 'a fundamental legacy
from their Communist past: the absence of the concept of a loyal opposition'.[4] Such reasoning assumes that conservative authoritarianism is
an external threat to the West, reversing the liberal-democratic transformation that had been exported eastward after 1990. To the extent that
the conservative-nationalist PiS and its leader, Jaroslaw Kaczyński, capi-
talizing on the sleaze and inequalities of the PO's two terms in power,
have mobilized 'good Christian Poles' against the country's corrupt
political caste, seen as linked to the more powerful international elites
in Brussels, Berlin and Moscow, the PiS project is aptly described by
contemporary usages of the term 'populist', meaning any political movement that challenges the liberal consensus.[5]

The predominant approach, as developed by Dutch political scientist Cas
Mudde, treats populism as a 'thin' moralistic ideology, according to which
the central political divide is that between a 'pure people' and 'corrupt
elite'. Populist opposition to globalization, or to the US–EU liberal consensus, also raises the problem theorized by Fareed Zakaria in the 1990s, with
reference to Bosnia, Pakistan and the Philippines: that democracy and liberalism are not the same thing: 'democracy is flourishing; constitutional
liberalism is not', Zakaria warned. Popularly elected governments might
ignore the constitutional limits on power and diminish the independent
institutions of the state, fostering 'illiberal democracies'.[6] Applied to the
Polish case, such an interpretation reveals some real and important features of PiS rule. However, it also rests upon two presuppositions which
need to be tested. First, that the political order accompanying the return
to capitalism in Poland after 1989 itself operated upon liberal-democratic

---

[4] Sierakowski, 'The Polish Threat to Europe', *Social Europe*, 16 Jan 2016.
[5] Marco D'Eramo, 'Populism and the New Oligarchy', NLR 82, Jul–Aug 2013. For a
nuanced discussion of the interplay of 'community' and 'democracy' in contemporary Polish political culture, see Leszek Koczanowicz, 'The Polish Case', NLR 102,
Nov–Dec 2016.
[6] See Cas Mudde and Cristóbal Rovira Kaltwasser, *Populism: A Very Short
Introduction*; Fareed Zakaria, 'The Rise of Illiberal Democracy', *Foreign Affairs*, Nov–
Dec 1997; see also Mudde, 'The Populist Zeitgeist', *Government and Opposition*,
vol. 39, no. 4, pp. 541–63, drawing on Zakaria.

principles. Second, that PiS rule is a regime of pure regression—and thus a rupture, not to say an aberration, from post-transition Polish politics. What follows will briefly examine each in turn.

A democratic transition?

The origins of Poland's reintegration into international capital markets can be traced to the mid-1970s, when the Gierek government began taking cheap 'petro-dollar' loans from Western banks. By the end of the decade, these creditors were pressing Warsaw to expand exports and reduce subsidies on consumer goods—a contributing factor to the mass Solidarność strikes of 1980. The transition to capitalism in Poland can be dated to the crushing of the trade-union movement by martial law under Gen. Jaruzelski in 1981; henceforth, consumer prices rose and real wages fell. By the mid-80s, with a green light from Moscow given by Gorbachev's perestroika, the ruling Polish United Workers' Party was actively preparing for a transition, implementing a series of market reforms and taking the country into the World Bank and IMF. The 1989 Round Table talks, negotiating the transfer of political power between the Jaruzelski regime and the Solidarność opposition, initially agreed on a 'social-market economy'. Yet when a young Jerzy Sachs arrived in Warsaw in April 1989, the blueprint for liberal-economic shock therapy in his briefcase was wholeheartedly welcomed by the former left-wing Solidarność intellectuals as well as the modernizing *nomenklatura*. In December 1989, without any real debate or public consultation, Finance Minister Leszek Balcerowicz rammed a package of sixteen bills through the largely appointed Sejm—this was nearly two years before the first full parliamentary election—paving the way for the privatization of state-owned enterprises and elimination of price controls and subsidies. Poland's large working class bore the brunt of a huge surge in unemployment, poverty and inequality.[7]

In contrast to Russia and Ukraine, the advent of capitalism in Poland did not involve a transfer of public wealth to a homegrown oligarchy. Instead, huge swathes of the productive and financial sectors were transferred to foreign capital.[8] Balcerowicz pushed through rapid sales of assets, in

---

[7] Tadeusz Kowalik, *From Solidarity to Sell-Out: The Restoration of Capitalism in Poland*, New York 2012.
[8] For the role of the IMF, World Bank and European Commission in overseeing the break-up of Comecon trade relations, under US direction, see Peter Gowan, 'Neo-Liberal Theory and Practice for Eastern Europe', NLR 1/213, Sept–Oct 1995.

some instances for as little as 10 per cent of estimated value. By the end of the 1990s, foreign capital controlled 35 per cent of Poland's industrial stock, 70 per cent of its banking assets and 80 per cent of its print media.[9] The transfer of ownership through successive privatization programmes took place through the courts and state bureaucracies, shielded from public view. This was especially fraught in the case of property privatizations: incoherent laws left it up to the courts to rule on the forcible removal of tenants from their homes and the transfer of public spaces and buildings to private investors.[10] A major beneficiary of this process was the Church, awarded generous subsidies and grants of land that enabled it to build an extensive network of Catholic schools, universities and media outlets, becoming once again the largest private landowner in the country. Religious instruction was restored in schools without consulting parliament and abortion was criminalized, ignoring a petition signed by 1.5 million citizens demanding a referendum on the issue. In 1993 the Church's privileges were written into law via a Concordat with the Vatican, signed by the outgoing Suchocka administration without parliamentary scrutiny, and not ratified by the Sejm until 1998. The Church—an intrinsically secretive and authoritarian institution—thereby amassed huge wealth and political clout in the newly capitalist Poland.

In other words, most of the major strategic decisions concerning the country's post-communist course were taken without any real democratic consultation or mandate. The political order that oversaw the installation of economic liberalism in Poland was itself a form of non-accountable authoritarianism, though supported by liberal democrats in Poland and the West. It can be described as a type of 'undemocratic liberalism', under which non-elected authorities—including the IMF and European Commission, but also domestic players in the Central Bank and Finance Ministry—ensured that the range of issues available for democratic decision-making was sharply restricted, and responsibility for the most important political choices was handed over to financial institutions and other 'independent' authorities.

Ironically, Poland's 'undemocratic liberalism' was reinforced by its avowedly liberal-democratic political structures. In 1997, the country's

---

[9] Kazimierz Poznański, *Wielki Przekręt: Klęska Polskich Reform* [The Great Scam: Defeat of Polish Reforms], Warsaw 1999; Gavin Rae, *Poland's Return to Capitalism: From the Socialist Bloc to the European Union*, London 2012.
[10] Beata Siemieniako, *Reprywatyzując Polskę: Historia Wielkiego Przekrętu* [Reprivatizing Poland: History of the Great Scam], Warsaw 2017.

new constitution locked in 'German' macro-economic principles: public debt must not exceed 60 per cent of GDP, budget deficits cannot be financed by the Central Bank. The Constitution was put to a referendum, boycotted by the Solidarność trade union, that saw a turnout of only 43 per cent, of whom barely half approved it. There was no popular consultation on joining NATO in 1999, and only a minority of the electorate, some 42 per cent, endorsed accession to the European Union in 2004.[11] The electoral system, based on multi-member constituencies and the D'Hondt method of vote allocation—designed to boost the seats of winning parties, thereby distorting the representation of the popular will in favour of a 'stabilized' two-party system—has ensured that large numbers of Poles go unrepresented.[12] Turnout in parliamentary elections has been consistently low, averaging less than 50 per cent until 2019. Fewer than 1 per cent of the Polish electorate are members of a political party, the lowest share in any European Union country after Latvia, and only one in ten workers belongs to a trade union.[13]

This modus operandi had the support of the most important sections of the Polish intelligentsia, including the influential *Gazeta Wyborcza*, edited by former Solidarność theorist Adam Michnik, now extremely rich. Given the largely foreign ownership of Polish assets, and therefore the absence of a genuine business class, the Polish intelligentsia has stood in under the new capitalist order as a surrogate bourgeoisie. Its role during the Communist era had already equipped this stratum and its offspring with the cultural capital required to fill the upper ranks of a reconstituted class society, transmitting its understanding of Western values and lifestyles to those below; now it began to acquire real capital as well. The presiding outlook has been captured by Ivan Krastev as a 'culture of imitation': the West was simply the best. For Poland to become a 'normal' country, the residues of *homo sovieticus* would need to be replaced by the 'civilizational competencies' embodied in the European

---

[11] The EU accession referendum saw a turnout of 57 per cent of the electorate, 77 per cent of whom voted Yes; a victory achieved only with the help of the Pope, in return for Miller's government leaving the abortion ban in place.
[12] In 2015, PiS won 51 per cent of seats in the Sejm with the votes of roughly 20 per cent of the overall electorate—that is, 38 per cent of the vote on a 51 per cent turnout. The PO governments elected in 2007 and 2011 likewise won 45 per cent of the Sejm's seats with the support of a fifth of the electorate.
[13] See Ingrid van Biezen, 'The Decline in Party Membership', LSE European Politics Blog, 6 May 2013; Michał Feliksiak, 'Członkostwo w Związkach Zawodowych' [Membership in Trade Unions], CBOS, Warsaw, May 2013.

Union.[14] In 2007, a satisfied Michnik praised his fellow intellectuals for supporting the neoliberal reforms of the 90s and 2000s, resulting in the best period in Poland for more than three centuries, with a characteristic quip: 'every nation has the intelligentsia that it deserves, however I believe that our nation has a better intelligentsia than it deserves.'[15]

Even if 'undemocratic' in its installation, hasn't economic liberalization proved itself in practice? Yes and no. For the West, Poland was the jewel in the Comecon crown and received unstinting support from the IMF and EU, becoming the first CEE country to recover its pre-transition level of GDP. It has since seen a prolonged period of economic growth, its GDP per capita increasing by almost 150 per cent since 1989.[16] Any visitor to Warsaw will find a country changed beyond recognition over the past thirty years: this is no longer a society gazing enviously over the Iron Curtain at the glistening goods, music and fashion out of reach. The population is now as integrated into the global economy as that of Western Europe. Yet foreign investment has overwhelmingly targeted the high-end service economy of the capital and the western regions. Poland's eastern regions, dominated by small-scale agriculture and deindustrialized towns, are among the poorest in the EU; GDP per capita is 82 per cent of the EU average in Greater Warsaw, but less than 40 per cent of it in the east.[17] Across the country, public infrastructure is largely the legacy of the communist era. Unemployment has fallen from the high levels of the 1990s, partly due to mass emigration—over 2 million Poles have left to work abroad since EU accession in 2004—but precarity has increased: by 2012 over a quarter of the workforce was on temporary contracts, while the proportion of young Poles with higher education in casual jobs had risen to 39 per cent. Streams of Polish graduates

---

[14] See respectively, Tomasz Zarycki et al., 'The Roots of Polish Culture-Centred Politics', *East European Politics and Societies*, vol. 31, no. 2, 2017; Ivan Krastev and Stephen Holmes, 'Explaining Eastern Europe: Imitation and Its Discontents', *Journal of Democracy*, vol. 29, no. 3, July 2018; Agata Pyzik, *Poor but Sexy*, London 2014. For 'competencies', see Piotr Sztompka, 'Civilizational Incompetence: The Trap of Post-Communist Societies', *Zeitschrift für Soziologie*, vol. 22, no. 2, 1993.
[15] Adam Michnik, 'Mowa pogrzebowa nad grobem IV Rzeczypospolitej' [Funeral Speech over the Tomb of the Fourth Polish Republic], *Gazeta Wyborcza* supplement, 31 December 2007.
[16] Marcin Piątkowski, *Europe's Growth Champion: Insights from the Economic Rise of Poland*, Oxford 2018.
[17] Piotr Bogumil, 'Regional Disparities in Poland', ECFIN *Country Focus*, vol. 6, no. 4, 18 May 2009.

continued to leave the country for menial jobs in London, Dublin or Berlin. All was not well.

Preconditions

How, in this context, should we understand the rise of the conservative-nationalist PiS regime? Should its record be seen as a pure regression from post-transition Polish politics? Two developments paved the way for the rise of Kaczyński's PiS. The first was the elimination of a credible governing party on the left. The 'post-communist' Democratic Left Alliance (SLD), incorporating the younger, more liberal currents of the old ruling party, enjoyed a relatively successful term in office in the mid-1990s, as Poland began to recover from shock therapy. In 1997 it lost to a coalition of Solidarność conservatives, then returned to power in 2001 on a promise to restore social spending, winning 41 per cent of the vote.[18] Once in office, however, the SLD leadership, President Aleksander Kwaśniewski and Prime Minister Leszek Miller, deepened the neoliberal course to meet the accession criteria laid down by the EU, while the Central Bank and Monetary Policy Council kept interest rates high, strengthening the złoty while stunting economic growth. Miller and Kwaśniewski were eager recruits to the short-lived triumphalism of Blair's Third Way, joining the occupations of Afghanistan and Iraq, and hosting secret CIA prisons on Polish soil. They cynically abandoned a pledge to liberalize the abortion law in order to get Church backing for the EU referendum. Increasingly unpopular, the SLD's ratings plunged as a series of corruption scandals came to light over the sale of state assets and media regulation. The political fallout was severe and long-lasting. In 2005, with turnout down to barely 41 per cent, the SLD slumped to 11 per cent, with just 1.3 million votes, while the PiS and PO soared to 3.1 million and 2.8 million, respectively. Since then, a chastened and diminished SLD has shrunk to the ranks of a minor political player, its fate reinforced by the D'Hondt electoral system; even in coalition with other left fractions, it has struggled to win more than 10 per cent of Sejm seats.

The decimation of the SLD left the field open to the right-wing parties that had emerged out of the post-Solidarność bloc: the contest between

---

[18] Albeit the turnout in the 2001 parliamentary election was only 46 per cent, so the SLD's '41 per cent', or 5.3 million votes, amounted to the actual support of only 18 per cent of the electorate; the combined vote of the two newly formed parties of the right, the PO and PiS, was 2.8 million.

PO and PiS has dominated Polish politics ever since. PO is historically derived from a Communist-era intellectual current known as the Gdańsk liberals, Hayekians who criticized the Solidarność movement for its overemphasis on democracy and socialist economics. One of their number, Donald Tusk, a former student leader at the University of Gdańsk, stated that he would prefer capitalism without democracy to socialism with democracy.[19] During the 1990s, the group participated in a number of post-Solidarność administrations, promulgating a Thatcherite mix of neoliberal economics and social conservatism. The PiS founders, including Jarosław Kaczyński and his twin brother Lech, sprang mainly from another minority current within Solidarność. Fervently anti-Communist, they gained some influence within conservative sections of the intelligentsia through their close connections to the Catholic Church. In the early 1990s, both strands converged around the notion that a new elite, insufficiently purged of Communists, had usurped political power; both drew upon the tradition of the interwar strongman Józef Piłsudski and his Sanacja campaign to cleanse the Polish state. By the turn of the millennium, however, Tusk had repositioned himself and the newly founded PO as firmly pro-EU and free-market, promising to take Poland to the heart of Europe. The 2005 presidential election, pitting Tusk against Lech Kaczyński, went to the PiS candidate, while the 2007 parliamentary elections went to PO.

The second pre-condition for the rise of PiS was thus the ignominious collapse of PO. In office from 2007 to 2014, Tusk benefited from huge inflows of EU funds, producing the visible but highly uneven growth noted above, and in 2011 won an unprecedented second term. Yet the 'Polish boom' also raised social expectations: people could see the new wealth that was being created and expected to share in the success. When this was not forthcoming, frustration and hostility grew—exacerbated by Tusk's second-term assault upon the public sector: over 150 public hospitals were shut down, along with a thousand primary schools; public-housing construction was halved; controversial changes to the state-pension system raised the retirement age to 67. Simultaneously, PO ministers and their wealthy media friends were indulging in the ostentatious displays of wealth enjoyed by the jet-setting Sikorski and Applebaum. While attempting to court popularity with a hard-line conservative stance on abortion, LGBT rights and nationalist historiography, the PO had become embroiled in corruption scandals and now rapidly

---

[19] Rafał Kalukin, 'Donald Tusk: Kariera brata łaty', *Gazeta Wyborcza*, 14 Oct 2005.

lost popularity, even as it tried to push through a series of political appointments to the judiciary.

Meanwhile the mood of the country had darkened after the tragedy of the 2010 Smolensk air crash; the 96 victims, among them many leading figures from the Polish state, included President Lech Kaczyński, en route to commemorate the wartime massacre of Polish officers by Stalin in the Katyń Forest. The symbolic parallels with 1940 opened up deep historical wounds in Polish society and provided fertile ground for elements of the conservative right to develop conspiracy theories of collusion between the Tusk, Putin and Merkel governments. It also consolidated a strong emotional bond between Jarosław Kaczyński and the core PiS electorate, providing a crucible for the fusion of Catholic conservatism, anti-Communism, and hostility to Russia and Germany, combined.

It was in this context that Kaczyński promised to cleanse the state of a corrupt cosmopolitan elite on behalf of the people, the real Poles, those who had stood for generations against the country's occupiers. The flimsiness of this historical myth was of little importance. What mattered was that PiS offered to right the injustices of the previous quarter of a century. For the first time, a government in Warsaw would represent the interests of the 'losers' of the transition, stand up to the elites at home and abroad, and not treat the traditions of its nation as if they were something to be ashamed of. Kaczyński was strongly critical of Poland's subservient position within the international economy. He pledged to raise taxes on large, mostly foreign-owned banks and corporations, increase welfare spending and restore the previous retirement age. This stance saw the PiS candidate, Duda, win the presidential election in May 2015. The parliamentary elections of October 2015 came at the height of the hubbub over refugees in Europe, and Kaczyński promoted an Islamophobia which had not previously been openly expressed in mainstream public debate. On polling day, PiS was the clear victor, with 38 per cent of the vote and 235 seats.[20]

For the position of Prime Minister, Kaczyński initially selected the party's deputy leader, Beata Szydło, who embodied the pro-family image that PiS was trying to craft. Though Kaczyński is the undisputed leader of PiS—standing at the head of a patrimonial structure whereby party

---

[20] Again, the 2015 turnout was only 51 per cent, and the PiS popular vote at 5.7 million was an underwhelming 20 per cent of the overall electorate.

and government are held together through personal fealty to the chief—
he does not hold any formal governmental position, leaving him free
to conduct affairs from the side-lines as an ordinary MP. He has constructed an unusual form of anti-charismatic leadership, appearing not
to court public approval and presenting an image that is the antithesis of
the polished post-political style of his liberal-conservative rivals. At the
same time, he has constructed an effective personality cult around his
twin brother, the former President, who lies buried in Kraków's Wawel
Castle, next to Piłsudski. Statues of Lech Kaczyński have been erected
around the country, with another added recently in central Warsaw; the
symbolism of Smolensk—of noble Polish suffering—remains strong.

Record in office

To what extent, then, does the Kaczyński regime's record in office represent a rupture with what came before? In economic policy, the most
significant change has been in welfare. Szydło introduced a number of
social reforms, including lowering the pension age and implementing a
new package of child benefits, known as 500+, targeting large families
where child poverty was disproportionately high. It had an immediate
positive effect, child poverty falling from 23 per cent to 11 per cent in
just two years. The number of children with access to benefits nearly
doubled, from 2 million to 3.8 million.[21] This provided a new source
of income for a wide range of social groups, including many from the
middle class, thus cementing support for PiS across a broad spectrum of
society. In its cultural conservatism, 500+ represented a continuity with
the previous PO regime: the policy aimed to promote a traditional role
for women, who were encouraged to stay at home and have children. It
has failed on its own terms, contributing to a fall in female labour-force
participation without increasing the birth rate; it uses funds that could
be better spent on developing public infrastructure such as nurseries. In
purely redistributive terms, however, if 500+ represents a rupture with
neoliberal orthodoxy, it was not clear that it was a regression. PiS has
shown that it is able to deliver on a social promise without succumbing
to domestic and EU warnings that such profligacy would result in an
economic catastrophe.

---

[21] Ryszard Szarfenberg, 'Wpływ świadczenia wychowawczego (500+) na ubóstwo
ogółem i ubóstwo dzieci na podstawie mikrosymulacji' [Impact of Child Benefit
(500+) on Total and Child Poverty, Micro-Simulation], University of Warsaw,
24 February 2017.

The markets have largely priced the PiS regime as one of continuity, after an initial blip in 2015 when Standard and Poor's cut the country's rating, citing concerns about the political situation. They needn't have worried. Despite a tax on some assets of private banks, PiS postponed a proposal to tax large supermarkets, and left the country's regressive business and income tax rates well alone. Two years into PiS's first term, Kaczyński replaced Szydło with Mateusz Morawiecki, an economist and technocrat with over two decades' experience in financial institutions in Poland and Germany. Financial capital gave its stamp of approval, Poland becoming the first post-Communist nation to be ranked as a developed country by the FTSE Russell Index. Ironically, generous inflows of funds from the 2014–21 EU budget negotiated by Tusk have allowed PiS to increase public spending. With annual GDP growth of 5 per cent in 2017 and 2018, and foreign investment expanding at its fastest rate since the global financial crisis, Poland won praise as 'Europe's growth champion'. The number of Poles with wealth worth over 1 million złoty rose by a fifth in a single year.[22] Meanwhile the only sector of the economy to see a significant expansion of state investment has been the arms industry, with the Ministry of Defence taking over the Polish Armaments Group in order to increase production: Kaczyński has pledged to raise military spending to 2.5 per cent of GDP, above the NATO average. Otherwise, he has largely been content to fill the top positions of government companies with his own people.

The main complaints from Western observers like Garton Ash and Applebaum have focused on PiS interventions in the judiciary and media. On the first, it's worth noting that, in contrast to Western Europe and the US, there is a high degree of scepticism about the judiciary in Poland. In one survey, only a fifth of Poles believed that the courts and prosecutor's office were working well, with most stating that they were inefficient and corrupt.[23] The current battle over appointments began in 2015 under the outgoing PO government, when PM Kopacz attempted to pack the Constitutional Court with new judges ahead of elections which she was clearly going to lose. Duda refused to swear them in, and when shortly afterwards PiS took control of the Sejm it selected judges of its own and refused to publish Constitutional Court rulings countermanding the appointments. Since then, PiS has taken the process further—a

---

[22] Piątkowski, *Europe's Growth Champion*.
[23] 'CBOS: tylko jedna piąta Polaków dobrze ocenia funkcjonowanie sądów' [CBOS: Only a fifth of Poles positively assess functioning of courts], *Wiadomości*, 14 Jan 2013.

deepening of, rather than a rupture with, its predecessor's practice. The Justice Minister, Zbigniew Ziobro—now also Prosecutor General—was given new powers over the common courts and fired one in five court presidents. Lowering the retirement age of Supreme Court justices from seventy to sixty-five, albeit in line with national policy, removed a third of its members, including the Chief Justice.

Supposedly neutral, the public broadcaster TVP had been largely supine under Tusk, operating as an informal wing of the state—not unlike the BBC. Kaczyński and his circle expected no less for their own world outlook. Garton Ash cites an analysis in the run-up to this summer's presidential election: for the period 3–16 June 2020, 97 per cent of TVP stories about Duda were positive; 87 per cent of stories about Trzaskowski were negative, earning it the nickname of TVPiS; he concedes, however, that public TV has always been inclined to sway under pressure from the governing parties.[24]

The nationalist discourse of the PiS has continued a rightist historical revisionism that originated in previous PO administrations—though again, it has been amplified. In place of liberal emulation of the West, Kaczyński sees Poland as one of the last bastions defending a Christian Europe against the 'cultural Marxist' policies of multiculturalism infecting the West. PiS has intensified an existing campaign of de-communization, for example changing street names honouring left-wing historical figures, such as the Communist battalion that fought against Nazi occupation during the Warsaw Uprising.[25] New national heroes have been created to replace them. Yet the proposal for an annual National Remembrance Day to honour the 'cursed' soldiers who took up arms against Communist rule after World War Two, some of them responsible for mass civilian killings, actually originated from PO-supported President Bronisław Komorowski in 2010 and passed through parliament while Tusk was in office. The PiS is undoubtedly emboldening the small far-right parties, which up till now had negligible electoral support. The Independence Day march on 11 November used to be a tiny far-right affair, but its numbers have swelled. In 2018, the centenary of Polish independence, around 200,000 people joined the march after it effectively merged with the official celebrations addressed by President Duda.

---

[24] Garton Ash, 'For a Bitter Taste of Polish Populism, Just Watch the Evening News'.
[25] Many of the changes have been annulled by court rulings that the old place names did not, in fact, conflict with the constitutional prohibition of totalitarian ideology.

In many ways, PiS has not so much reversed Poland's political direction of travel as stepped down harder on the accelerator. Many of its more retrograde policies had already fermented in the national political culture before it came to power. The political and economic empowering of the Catholic Church in the 1990s had already provided the conservative right with significant institutional and ideological resources, while the anti-Communist rhetoric and historical revisionism of the PO between 2007 and 2015 cleared the way for Kaczyński. A regressive taxation system, the fashion for combining business with politics, and a pro-American foreign policy have all been consistent features of the national scene for many years. Poland's draconian anti-abortion laws were pushed through by the Solidarność right in the early 1990s. In 2016, Szydło's government allowed the introduction of a bill to ban abortion even when the woman's life is at risk or in cases of rape. This triggered a massive outpouring of anger against the government, with so-called 'black protests'—demonstrators dressed in black clothing as a symbol of mourning—organized around the country, which eventually succeeded in getting the bill dropped.[26]

Second, while many elements of PiS's programme are reactionary and anti-left, it also offers an expansion of social welfare and continued economic development. In this sense, to dismiss it as a regime of regression is to overlook the modernizing, mass-democratic appeal of its political project. This indicates one reason why the early mass mobilizations against the Kaczyński regime have not led to a political movement that could seriously challenge it. Dissent has largely been confined to a relatively privileged urban milieu, some of whose representatives publicly disparage the poorer social layers that sustain PiS in power. A well-known liberal professor alleged that in the district where she lives, there are families who keep small children in drawers because they do not own a bed, and that when they receive social help, they would rather spend the money on alcohol. One of Poland's most famous actresses has compared PiS voters to prostitutes who have sold themselves for social-welfare handouts.[27] The October 2019 parliamentary election put this

[26] Agnieszka Wiśniewska, 'The Black Protests Have Changed Poland', FES Connect, 18 March 2018.
[27] Cezary Michalski, 'Środa: PiS to bolszewicka metoda polityczna w służbie prawicowej kulturalnej wojny' [Środa: PiS is a Bolshevik political method in the culture wars], Krytyka Polityczna, 15 February 2016; 'Wybory 2019. Krystyna Janda podała kontrowersyjny wpis. Wyborcy PiS porównani z prostytutkami' [Election 2019. Krystyna Janda's controversial intervention. PiS voters compared to prostitutes],

to the test. Kaczyński launched the campaign pledging to extend 500+ benefits to all children and raise the minimum wage. He also rekindled the PIS's culture war, claiming that the traditional Polish way of life was under threat from 'LGBT ideology'.[28] On a record turnout of 62 per cent, the PIS vote rose to 8 million, or 44 per cent of the vote—six points higher than in 2015. The party's position in the Sejm (235 seats) was unchanged. It won the largest share of the vote amongst all age groups and in all but two of the country's 16 voivodeships. The opposition coalition (KO), led by the PO, trailed behind on 27 per cent. The July 2020 presidential election confirms the PIS lead, albeit by a smaller margin.

What of the Polish left? With the political field polarized between conservative nationalists and liberal conservatives, it has been weakened by the logic of lesser evilism: in 2019 some sections, including the Greens and the current around United Left leader Barbara Nowacka, were absorbed into the PO's electoral coalition. Other figures argued for an even-handed opposition to the two major conservative parties: the writer Rafał Woś gave a positive assessment of the social policies of the government and urged the left to maintain its independence from PO, while his critics countered that 'symmetrism' downplays the dangers of PIS's authoritarian project.[29] In the event, two smaller groups—the radical-left Razem (Together) and Wiosna (Spring), a new social-liberal network—formed an electoral bloc, Lewica (The Left), with the SLD. Lewica took 13 per cent of the vote and 49 seats. Amongst its new MPs are some genuine left-wing activists from a younger generation that has helped to rebuild small political communities over the past decade and a half. These new currents had adopted a hostile attitude towards the SLD, seeing it as the major obstacle to building a strong left in Poland. But this position became increasingly unsustainable in conditions where the right has almost total political control. The SLD has, at least for the time being, adopted a more social-democratic programme and retains an electoral base, accounting for half of Lewica's new MPs. Yet despite some pockets of support, it is almost entirely absent in rural and eastern regions of the country;

Wiadomości, 15 October 2019. Anecdotes of parents spending the 500+ benefit on alcohol are not supported by the research, which shows that most of it has been spent on clothes, food and holidays for their children.
[28] A majority of Poles now favour legalizing same-sex civil unions, but not marriage or adoption. Anton Ambroziak, 'Rekordowe poparcie dla związków partnerskich i równości małżeńskiej' [Record support for civil unions and marital equality], *OKO.press*, 25 February 2019.
[29] Rafał Woś, *Lewicę racz nam zwrócić, Panie!* [Give Us Back Your Left Hand, Lord!] Katowice 2019.

instead, it competes with the PO for urban professionals' support in the big cities. The challenge it faces is to oppose the government's authoritarian agenda without being consumed by the liberal right.

This is not to say that PiS will remain invincible. Perhaps the most significant threat lies in the rumbling corruption scandals involving property and business dealings connected to leading PiS politicians—and, in the case of one development, Kaczyński himself.[30] The Health Minister, Lukasz Szumowski, is tangled up in accusations of over-spending on masks for the COVID pandemic, involving a crony of his brother. In addition, Poland's economic performance has been heavily dependent on EU expenditure, of which the country is the largest net beneficiary. Europe's capitals are still haggling over the Commission's Budget for 2021–27, and steep cuts to the cohesion and agriculture funds haven't been ruled out. In relative terms the coronavirus has not hit Poland particularly badly, with just over 1,000 confirmed deaths by early June, although coal production in Silesia has recently been hampered by a spike in infections in the mines. The country is forecast to record the shallowest recession of any EU member state this year. Morawiecki produced a 300 billion złoty (€66 billion) coronavirus support package in April and is lobbying for a generous allocation of the Commission's recovery fund. All this, however, entails hostages to fortune.

For now, PiS's hold is secure. That there would be a reaction from the right to the way in which Poland was integrated into Western economic structures as a source of cheap labour and destination for foreign capital, as well as to the prevailing liberal culture of Western imitation, was predictable.[31] PiS is certainly more nationalist and conservative than most of its governing counterparts in Western Europe. Up to now, however, it has been less brutal in its actions than either Macron against the *gilets jaunes* or the Spanish state in Catalonia; any damage it has done to the 'European ideal' pales before what the Troika inflicted upon Greece. As the realities of twenty-first-century capitalism become increasingly harsh, perhaps what Poland mirrors back at its Cold War demiurges is indeed a 'normal' European country.

---

[30] 'Fallout from the Kaczynski Twin Towers scandal', *Euractiv*, 30 January 2019.
[31] David Ost described how the grievances of the Polish working class were being channelled away from class politics by conservative-nationalist elements in *The Defeat of Solidarity: Anger and Politics in Postcommunist Europe*, Ithaca NY 2005.

'Much of the commentary about populism focuses upon nativism, exclusion, racism and authoritarianism. Such analyses have trouble explaining that left populism that has brought millions into politics. Jorge Tamames shows us why left populism is still populism, and that to understand populism fully, we need to understand the left.'

- Mark Blyth, Brown University

'A fascinating study into our tumultuous times... underlining that the populist moment is not a passing aberration. Critical to any understanding of this age of upheaval.'

- Owen Jones

 LAWRENCE & WISHART
www.lwbooks.co.uk

ALICE MACKENZIE BAMFORD

Alice joined NLR in 2017, first as an intern and then as assistant editor. In a sense, it was home from home. In 1984—four years before she was born—her father, the sociologist Donald MacKenzie, had written a powerful analysis of US nuclear-war planning for NLR 1/148. Her mother, Caroline Bamford, had done her doctoral research on the British New Left, and Alice spoke of growing up with a shelf of old NLRs, appropriately mouse-nibbled, in her bedroom in their village home outside Edinburgh. She was a high-flier: a first in English from the University of Edinburgh, a Masters from Oxford and a Cambridge PhD in Criticism and Culture, passing the viva voce without corrections. We publish below extracts from her dazzling doctoral dissertation on mathematics and modern literature, which placed literary treatments of mathematics—Musil, Beckett, Mallarmé, Valéry, 'Oulipo', Stein—in dialogue with images of it constructed by mathematical manifestos. At Cambridge she convened a graduate seminar on literary theory and taught on the undergraduate English course. But, she said, she knew exactly how Wittgenstein felt about the place. In late 2016 she applied for an internship at Verso, where she pulled together ideas for a philosophy of science list—scouting, she laughingly put it, for the next Paul Feyerabend. Soon she migrated upstairs to NLR. Her first piece for the journal, 'In the Wake of Trilling', engaged Amanda Anderson's Bleak Liberalism in a fine and penetrating critique, adorned in Alice's beautifully queenly style: 'The term Victorian, while it has long ceased to be as pejorative as it was . . . is seldom unambiguously laudatory either'. Her next, 'Intaglio as Philosophy', found Bachelard labouring in the same trench as Bouvard and Pécuchet. There followed 'Counterperfomativity' (NLR 113), co-written with Donald, an elegant essay in which the 'misfires' theorized by Austinian language philosophy illuminate and problematize the operations of the mathematical models at the heart of financial-derivative markets. She was a scrupulous copy editor, happy to muck in with office life or plan after-work sorties; taking part in all the everyday discussions about texts and things. But swallows can get vertigo; Alice was vulnerable, too. A diagnosis of MS—unthinkably hard—came as a destabilizing blow, though she struggled on. She was living on the Whitmore Estate in East London, a spirited participant in the evening clapping and pot-banging that resounded from the balconies under lockdown. Her sense of solidarity was deep-rooted: during a spell at St Pancras Hospital, she found a role as interpreter for the migrant waifs and strays who'd swept up there. In the second week of May, a friend who went round to check she was alright found her in bed, at peace. Blithe spirit, the poet said: like an unbound joy whose race is just begun.

ALICE BAMFORD

MATHEMATICS AND

MODERN LITERATURE

Passages from 'Chalk and the Architrave'

AMMA, A STUDENT in Imre Lakatos's drama, *Proofs and Refutations*, suggests: 'Why not have mathematical critics just as you have literary critics, to develop mathematical taste by public criticism?'[1] Lakatos's drama is set in a mathematics classroom. The students are debating the proof of the Euler characteristic for polyhedra. *Proofs and Refutations* follows the journey of Euler's Theorem from its birth as naive conjecture through the mistakes and revolutions of nineteenth-century mathematics, to adulthood.[2] As they speed through a century of mathematical history, the students live Lakatos's lesson: rigour and proof are historically variable values and practices. *Proofs and Refutations* offers, too, an education in the value of error: mathematical knowledge develops by dialectical criticism.[3]

Lakatos's stated enemy was the 'formalist' philosophy of mathematics. In particular, he objected to the formalist *image* of mathematics, which equated mathematics with 'its formal axiomatic abstraction' and the philosophy of mathematics with metamathematics. In Lakatos's opinion, formalism was disconnecting mathematics not just from its philosophy but also from its history:

> According to the formalist concept of mathematics, there is no history of mathematics proper. Any formalist would basically agree with Russell's 'romantically' put but seriously meant remark, according to which Boole's *Laws of Thought* (1854) was 'the first book ever written on mathematics'.[4]

Mathematics further exempts itself from history, in Lakatos's view, by forced adherence to a particular style of writing. This 'Euclidean' or 'deductivist' style imposes a fixed structure on the presentation of mathematics: the text begins with a list of axioms, lemmas and/or definitions, this list is followed by the theorem, and the theorem is followed by the proof. Readers of mathematics are watching a 'conjuring act': the deductivist style enforces the dogma that 'all propositions are true and all inferences valid' and presents mathematics 'as an ever-increasing set of eternal, immutable truths'.[5]

By tearing the results from their heuristic context and hiding the mathematician's initial conjectures, the counter-examples and the work of proof-analysis, deductivist style enforces a sense of finality and steels itself against criticism. 'Deductivist style', Lakatos writes, 'hides the struggle, hides the adventure. The whole story vanishes, the successive tentative formulations of the theorem in the course of the proof-procedure are doomed to oblivion while the end result is exalted into sacred infallibility'. Lakatos advocates, instead, the adoption of a heuristic style, in which the text would tell the story of its own emergence: the adventure and struggle of conjecture, counter-examples, criticism and proof-analysis.[6]

These passages are drawn from the dissertation 'Chalk and the Architrave: Mathematics and Modern Literature', for which Alice MacKenzie Bamford was awarded the degree of Doctor of Philosophy by the University of Cambridge in 2015.

[1] Imre Lakatos, *Proofs and Refutations: The Logic of Mathematical Discovery*, ed. by John Worrall and Elie Zahar, Cambridge 1976, p. 98.

[2] Euler's Theorem: the conjecture that for all polyhedra the number of their vertices, V, minus the number of their edges, E, plus the number of their faces, F, is 2 ($V-E+F=2$).

[3] Lakatos summarised the process of dialectical criticism in his appendix to *Proofs and Refutations*. First, there is a primitive conjecture (the thesis) and a 'proof' is formed ('a rough thought-experiment or argument, decomposing the primitive conjecture into subconjectures or lemmas'). Then comes the antithesis: 'global' counter-examples are found that appear to undermine the primitive conjecture. The proof is re-examined in order to find the 'guilty lemma': the subconjecture that can account for the global counter-examples. The guilty lemma, which may have been hidden or misstated in the original proof, is now made into an explicit condition of the primitive conjecture. This is the synthesis: the improved conjecture, produced by proof-analysis, supersedes the primitive conjecture. Lakatos, *Proofs and Refutations*, p. 127; hereafter PR.

[4] PR, p. 142.   [5] PR, p. 142.   [6] PR, p. 142.

Gamma's suggested new genre—'mathematical criticism'—can be found in the form of mathematical manifestos, prefaces, parables and essays that mediate and frame the discipline's entanglement with that which it understands to be other than itself—the liminal genres of modern mathematics. These works of prescriptive and performative disciplinary criticism seek to shape mathematical 'taste' by 'public criticism'. Mathematical manifestos reinforce and reconfigure the links between the disciplinary self-construction of mathematics, the repertoire of cultural images of mathematics and the social structure in which mathematical knowledge is embedded. The metaphors and rhetorical strategies deployed in 'peri-mathematical' or threshold texts are mediators: translating mathematics out of the formal language of proof and into a network of historical and rhetorical entanglements. At the same time, mathematical manifestos mobilise the political conditions and cultural assumptions of the historical moments in which they were written. Traces of the discipline's social and cultural history—of the making of mathematical values like rigour and exactness—are inscribed in the manifesto's mathematical criticism.

Manifestos mark crucial moments in the nineteenth and twentieth-century history of mathematics. The introduction to Augustin-Louis Cauchy's 1821 textbook, the *Cours d'analyse*, is seen by many historians of mathematics as marking a disjuncture between the hugely productive but informal development of the calculus over the previous 150 years and the start of its formalisation. Hermann Weyl's 1921 'Über die neue Grundlagenkrise der Mathematik' was the single most trenchant response to the late nineteenth and early twentieth century 'foundations crisis', a crisis that was in a sense the consequence of a series of mathematical results that showed contradictions in, or inherent limits of, efforts at formalization. N. Bourbaki's 'L'Architecture des Mathématiques' (1948) was an enormously influential mid-twentieth century effort to re-found mathematics. 'Nicolas Bourbaki' was the collective pseudonym of a group of predominantly French mathematicians whose *Éléments de mathématique* was designed to be a self-contained reconstruction of the core elements of modern mathematics in largely formalized language.

3

Mathematical manifestos are works of polemic and performative disciplinary criticism that announce a new foundational programme in mathematics, break with the previous order and promote a certain image of mathematics and its history. There are, certainly, broad parallels between 'modernist mathematics' and other forms of cultural modernism: a rupture with tradition, a turn toward formalism, and a heightened self-reflexivity. As such, mathematical manifestos may be read alongside other examples of the genre—literary and artistic manifestos such as Marinetti's 'Technical Manifesto of Futurist Literature' (1912), Pound's 'Vorticism' (1914), Khlebnikov's 'To the Artists of the World!' (1919) and the Oulipo manifestos (1960–73) of François Le Lionnais, Raymond Queneau and Jacques Roubaud.

References to mathematics pervaded the manifestos of the European avant-gardes. The deployment of mathematics as an organizing metaphor and appeals to the epistemic virtues of mathematics are, indeed, common strategies in the construction of literary and artistic movements: Novalis's definition of Romanticism, T. E. Hulme's geometrical classicism, or the mathematical analogies of Pound's vorticist manifestos, for example. Just as the history of mathematics bears witness not to a 'royal road' to modern precision, exactness and foundational rigour, but rather to the cyclical, strategic deployment of calls to foundational retrenchment, rigour and formalism, so, too, does literary history reflect the cyclical and strategic deployment of mathematics as a cultural and symbolic resource at moments of disciplinary re-negotiation: Musil, Pound or Beckett.

4

Bourbaki's thunderbolt, the *Éléments de mathématique*, began its life as a somewhat modest, conventional project. Henri Cartan and André Weil were two young mathematicians responsible for teaching courses on differential and integral calculus at Strasbourg. In his memoir, Weil describes Cartan constantly complaining about the lack of a good analysis textbook and pestering Weil with questions about how to teach the calculus course. Weil proposed solving the problem for good: they would get a group of mathematicians together (friends of theirs who were teaching the same topics at various universities) and collectively write what they thought of as a new *Cours d'analyse*: a new analysis textbook. The group met on 10 December 1934 to discuss this 'Traité d'Analyse'. The minutes of this meeting record:

> WEIL presents his project—to establish the content of the certificate in differential and integral calculus for the next 25 years by jointly writing a treatise on analysis. It is agreed that this treatise will be as modern as possible.[7]

At the Committee's meeting on 14 January 1935, the analyst and functional theorist Szolem Mandelbrojt proposed 'un principe de généralité': that all the necessary general and abstract theories should be given at the beginning of the book. 'We must', Weil said, 'write a treatise that could be used by anyone: by researchers (university lecturers or not), by students, by future educators, by physicists and by all engineers'.[8] As such, the tools of mathematics were to be given in the most universal form. This abstract section grew until it engulfed the treatise on analysis. Bourbaki's project was reimagined as writing the 'ultimate mathematics textbook'.[9] Even the choice of title, *Éléments de mathématique*, was provocative: Bourbaki used '*mathématique*' in the singular (rather than the conventional *mathématiques*). An unpublished draft introduction opened on an even stronger note: 'THERE IS one mathematic, unique and indivisible: hence the rationale for the present treatise, which will expose the elements of it in the light of twenty-five centuries.'[10]

5

The name 'Bourbaki' today connotes mathematical structuralism and an austere, formalist, axiomatic style (and indeed, for those old enough to

---

[7] Réunion du 10/12/1934, Delta 001, *Archives de l'Association des Collaborateurs de Nicolas Bourbaki*. See also André Weil, *The Apprenticeship of a Mathematician*, trans. Jennifer Gage, Basel 1992, pp. 99–100.

[8] Réunion du 14/01/1935, Delta 002, pp. 2–3, *Archives de l'Association des Collaborateurs de Nicolas Bourbaki*.

[9] Leo Corry, 'Writing the Ultimate Mathematics Textbook: Nicolas Bourbaki's *Éléments de mathématique*', in Eleanor Robson and Jacqueline Stedall, eds, *The Oxford Handbook of the History of Mathematics*, Oxford 2009.

[10] 'R145. Introduction au Livre I (Etat 2: Nunke)', *Archives de l'Association des Collaborateurs de Nicolas Bourbaki*.

remember it, the short-lived, heavily set-theoretic 'New Math' of 1960s curriculum reform).[11] Yet both Bourbaki's structuralism and their axiomatic style were ambivalent, even contradictory. Bourbaki's structures led double lives. 'Structure' had both a formal and a nonformal meaning in their work.[12] Bourbaki's structuralist image of mathematics belongs above all to their peri-mathematical writing: to their histories, parables, prefaces and manifestos and, in particular, to 'The Architecture of Mathematics', written by Weil's friend Jean Dieudonné and published in a special issue of *Cahiers du Sud*, edited by François Le Lionnais, in 1948. Le Lionnais, chemical engineer, poet and mathematician, would republish the 'Architecture' in his two-volume *Great Currents of Mathematical Thought* (an encyclopaedic project that was never, in fact, completed).[13] He would go on to become a founding member of Oulipo and to write the first manifestos of the Oulipo movement.

Bourbaki's manifesto argues that, despite the apparent splitting of mathematics into specialized branches, the discipline can and will retain its unity. The 'axiomatic method' is Bourbaki's insurance against the threat of the discipline's fragmentation: against the possibility of mathematics becoming 'a tower of Babel of autonomous disciplines'. Bourbaki's axiomatic method enables 'a systematizing of the relations existing among the various mathematical theories'. Bourbaki's project will show the underlying unity of mathematics by a process of analysis and synthesis. Each theory will be decomposed into its constituent elements, and the relations among those elements will be uncovered and reordered into a hierarchy of types of mathematic 'structure'. As such, 'mathematical structures become, properly speaking, the *sole "objects"* of

---

[11] In Germany the backlash against the New Math made the cover of *Der Spiegel* on 25 March 1974: the headline 'Macht Mengenlehre krank?' ('Sickened by set theory?') was emblazoned across the face of an unhappy-looking child. In the United States, Morris Kline denounced the Bourbaki-inspired educational reforms in *Why Johnny Can't Add: The Failure of the New Math*, New York 1973.

[12] For the Israeli historian of mathematics, Leo Corry: 'On the one hand, ['structure'] suggested a general organizational scheme for the entire discipline, which turned out to be very influential. On the other hand, it comprised a concept that was meant to provide the underlying formal unity but was of no mathematical value whatsoever either within Bourbaki's own treatise or outside it': 'Writing the Ultimate Mathematics Textbook', p. 579.

[13] Bourbaki, 'The Architecture of Mathematics', in François Le Lionnais, ed., *Great Currents of Mathematical Thought, Vol. 1. Mathematics: Concepts and Development*, trans. R. A. Hall and Howard Bergman, New York 1971, pp. 23–37.

mathematics'. Bourbaki use two metaphors of modernization to explain their reconstruction project: Haussmann's Paris and Taylor's factory line. Mathematics, Bourbaki write, is:

> Like a great city whose suburbs never cease to grow in a somewhat cha-otic fashion on the surrounding lands, while its centre is periodically reconstructed, each time following a clearer plan and a more majestic arrangement, demolishing the old sections with their labyrinthine alleys in order to launch new avenues toward the periphery, always more direct, wider and more convenient.[14]

The axiomatic method enables, Bourbaki argue, an 'economy of thought': 'It can thus be said that the axiomatic method is nothing but the "Taylor System"—the "scientific management"—of mathematics'. Yet the factory-line metaphor proves inadequate, and Bourbaki immediately retract their claim: 'this comparison is not sufficiently close; the mathematician does not work mechanically as does the worker on the assembly line; the fundamental role that a special *intuition* plays in his research cannot be overestimated'.[15] The manifesto is full of moments of disavowal.

While proclaiming themselves the heirs to David Hilbert's math-ematical formalism, Bourbaki seek to absolve themselves from the charges levelled at formalism (that it is a 'lifeless skeleton', machine-like, divorced from physical reality, somehow inhuman) by deploying an organic register of biological language (they talk of organisms, 'mother-structures', 'nourishing sap' and so on) alongside the inor-ganic, modernist, often architectural register of structure and form. In fact, Bourbaki's biological language echoes Hilbert's own rhetoric. He, too, used the romanticist, biological metaphor of the organic whole to defend the unity of mathematics: 'Mathematical science is in my opin-ion an indivisible whole, an organism whose vitality is conditional upon the connection of its parts.'[16]

The manifesto's method of tropological substitution enables mathe-matical 'modernism' to co-exist with intuition, with romanticism, with the organic: in other words, with everything that modernism is said to have erased from mathematics. Bourbaki's project, the unification of

---

[14] Bourbaki, 'The Architecture of Mathematics', p. 34.
[15] Bourbaki, 'The Architecture of Mathematics', p. 31.
[16] David Hilbert, 'Mathematical Problems' [1902], trans. by M. W. Newson, *Bulletin of the American Mathematical Society* 8, pp. 478–9.

mathematics, is thus played out in their manifesto at the tropological level: the unity of mathematics is brought about—albeit uneasily—by the unification of images of mathematics and varying metaphors for mathematical unity. Indeed, Le Lionnais hinted at this discursive unification project in his commentary: 'Bourbaki's message, so rich and so dense with meaning, has as its overall aim a systematic inventory of the analogies in mathematics and at the same time an elucidation of their validity and of their significance'.[17]

6

In the introduction to their volume on set theory, Bourbaki invoked the rigour of the ancients to defend the essential stability of mathematics: the invariance of the discipline's paradigm of legitimacy and its concepts of proof and rigour, and—one is forced to add—an essentially Western (and not Babylonian, Indian, Chinese or Arabic) genealogy.[18] They write:

> Ever since the time of the Greeks, mathematics has involved proof; and it is even doubted by some whether proof, in the precise and rigorous sense which the Greeks gave to this word, is to be found outside mathematics. We may fairly say that this sense has not changed, because what constituted a proof for Euclid is still a proof for us; and in times when the concept has been in danger of oblivion, and consequently mathematics itself has been threatened, it is to the Greeks that men have turned again for models of proof. But this venerable bequest has been enlarged during the past hundred years by important acquisitions.[19]

Bourbaki sought to identify and to codify the essential, invariant aspects of mathematical language: 'By analysis of the mechanism of proofs in suitably chosen mathematical texts, it has been possible to discern the structure underlying both vocabulary and syntax.' Bourbaki claimed that proofs can always be recognized as proofs because, beneath the local variations in the surface layer of the text, they share an underlying structure. Yet, since the mathematical text is defined by its hypothetical formalization, the underlying structure of proof exists only in the realm of potentiality. In practice, mathematicians do not and cannot make

---

[17] Le Lionnais, ed., *Great Currents of Mathematical Thought*, Vol. *I*, p. 11.
[18] Compare, for example, Karine Chemla and Guo Shuchun, *Les neuf chapitres: Le classique mathématique de la Chine ancienne et ses commentaires*, Paris 2004.
[19] Bourbaki, *Elements of Mathematics: Theory of Sets* [1970], New York 2004, p. 7.

Leibniz's dream real: they never write out their proofs in an entirely formal language. Such a project would be, Bourbaki point out, 'absolutely unrealizable' as 'the tiniest proof at the beginning of the Theory of Sets would already require several hundreds of signs for its complete formalization'. Bourbaki, therefore, must appeal to their implied reader's 'intuition', to their 'common sense' and to their 'confidence'—'a confidence analogous to that accorded by a calculator or an engineer to a formula or a numerical table without any awareness of the existence of Peano's axioms'.[20]

The rigour of a proof is, nonetheless, judged on 'the possibility of translating it unambiguously into such a formalized language'. The arts of reading and of writing mathematics require a kind of double vision: 'Thus, written in accordance with the axiomatic method and keeping always in view, as it were on the horizon, the possibility of a complete formalization, our series lays claim to perfect rigour.' Bourbaki's mathematical structuralism sounds rather like linguistic structuralism here (they could be discussing the *langue* and *parole* of mathematical language), and indeed they reference linguistics in defence of their project:

> Just as the art of speaking a language correctly precedes the invention of grammar, so the axiomatic method had been practised long before the invention of formalized languages; but its conscious practice can rest only on the knowledge of the general principles governing such languages and their relationship with current mathematical texts.[21]

Bourbaki, however, were not concerned with 'languages' in the plural. Bourbaki describe their 'axiomatic method' as a way to transcend the limitations of specialization. When faced with 'complex mathematical objects', Bourbaki 'separate their properties'—algebraic properties,

---

[20] Bourbaki, *Elements of Mathematics: Theory of Sets*, pp. 7, 10–11. Peano's axioms are the canonical formalization of the natural numbers and thus of arithmetic.
[21] Bourbaki, *Elements of Mathematics: Theory of Sets*, pp. 8, 12, 9. Bourbaki's mathematical structuralism did occasionally cross paths with other structuralisms. André Weil, for example, worked with Claude Lévi-Strauss and wrote a mathematical appendix to Part One of *The Elementary Structures of Kinship*: 'On the algebraic study of certain types of marriage laws (Murngin system)'. For an extended analysis of Bourbaki's links with French structuralism, see David Aubin, 'The Withering Immortality of Nicolas Bourbaki: A Cultural Connector at the Confluence of Mathematics, Structuralism, and the Oulipo in France', *Science in Context*, vol. 10, no. 2, 1997, pp. 297–342.

topological properties, and so on—and 'regroup them around a small number of concepts': they 'classify them according to the *structures* to which they belong'. Indeed, where it was once thought that the results in each branch of mathematics were dependent on that branch's distinctive form of mathematical intuition, it is now, Bourbaki argue, logically possible 'to derive practically the whole of known mathematics from a single source, the Theory of Sets'. In light of this, Bourbaki give the principles of a single formalized language, and then specify how set theory 'could be written in this language', before showing how various other branches of mathematics might fit into their unified language project.

7

With its fictional author, the mysterious 'N. Bourbaki', and its grandiose proclamations, *Éléments de mathématique* was, as the Oulipo poet and mathematician Jacques Roubaud would write, a 'provocative and avant-gardist treatise'; even 'a sort of mathematical surrealism'.[22] Bourbaki's mathematical surrealism is perhaps most evident in the absurdist humour of their internal bulletin, *La Tribu*, 'the tribe', subtitled *Bulletin oecuménique apériodique et bourbachique*. While the humour of *La Tribu* tends towards a kind of surrealism, Bourbaki's treatise and their manifesto, 'The Architecture of Mathematics', reveal the group's affiliations with other valences of the avant-garde: with formalism, with revolutionary ambition, with modernist utopianism, with the *mathesis universalis* and other universal language projects, and with the desire to create an autonomous, unified work of art.

Formal experimentalism was equally evident in their historiographic method. 'Historical Notes' were appended to many of the chapters of Bourbaki's treatise. The 'Directions for Use' explains the rationale for the bracketing-off of history from mathematics proper:

> Since in principle the text consists of the dogmatic exposition of a theory, it contains in general no references to the literature. Bibliographical references are gathered together in *Historical Notes*, usually at the end of each chapter. These notes also contain indications, where appropriate, of the unsolved problems of the theory.[23]

---

[22] Jacques Roubaud, 'Mathematics in the Method of Raymond Queneau', p. 80.
[23] Bourbaki, *Elements of Mathematics: Theory of Sets*, p. vi.

In fact, rather than useful collections of references, these histories are strange pieces of prose, markedly different in style from the rest of the text: often highly subjective, sometimes lyrical, they oscillate between hagiography of individual, proto-modern mathematicians and appeals to the unstoppable, de-individualized force of ideas. Bourbaki's historical notes often spanned a wide expanse of time: sometimes reaching all the way back to the ancient Greeks or to the Babylonians. They tended to give the history of mathematics as the prehistory of Bourbaki.

A 1947 *La Tribu* invented the incident of a mock-historical report given as a supposed-inaugural speech in order to poke fun at both algebra and the style of Bourbaki's historiography:

> The historical note to chapters 2–3 of the *Algebra*, read in the guise of an inaugural address, put the congress 'in the right mood' for algebra: it glorified Fermat, obediently followed the meandering of the linear and examined the influence of Mallarmé on Bourbaki.[24]

Paradoxically, the strictures of axiomatic style that were imposed on Bourbaki's treatise also generated the semantic excesses of *La Tribu*: an overflow of non-formal, playful language; of pastiche, parody, puns, nonsense and poetry, in which words grabbed the multiple meanings they were denied in the *Éléments*. Bourbaki's absurdist sense of humour, hidden in their archives, is missing from many characterizations of the group. Roubaud, for example, claimed that the Oulipo were at once 'an homage to Bourbaki' and 'a parody of Bourbaki, even a profanation of Bourbaki', since:

> Bourbaki's initial plan—to rewrite Mathematics in its entirety and provide it with solid foundations using a single source, Set Theory, and a rigorous system, the Axiomatic Method—is at once serious, admirable, imperialistic, sectarian, megalomaniac, and pretentious. (Humour has not been one of its prime characteristics.)[25]

Yet the issues of Bourbaki's bulletin were full of jokes, nonsensical stories, hoaxes, neologisms and ridiculous anecdotes about the various

[24] *La Tribu: Bulletin oecuménique, apériodique et bourbachique*, 'Compte-rendu du Congrès de Noël' [1947], Archives Bourbaki.
[25] Jacques Roubaud, 'The Oulipo and Combinatorial Art' [1991], in Harry Mathews et al., eds, *Oulipo Compendium*, London 2005.

Bourbaki congresses. Many Bourbaki members were *normaliens*, and *La Tribu* abounds with the particular slang and the *canular* humour of the École Normale. Even the lists of members present at the Bourbaki congresses were defiantly odd: they sometimes included 'extras' (wives, children, locals, farm animals, etc.) and 'props' (cars, bicycles, prams, binoculars, aspirin, and other paraphernalia were listed alongside standards like the blackboard and its duster). Issues of *La Tribu* were also scattered with poetry: pastiches of, for example, Valéry or Mallarmé, that created a mythic genealogy for the figure of Bourbaki, or gave a mock-heroic account of his past triumphs.

La Tribu was often self-parodic. Issue 29, the report from the 'Congrès de l'incarnation de l'Ane qui trotte' is one such example: the incarnated 'trotting donkey' is a plodding mathematical exposition, and the report heaps further scorn upon Bourbaki's style in a satirical ballad. This *chanson paillarde* is to be sung, its author suggests, to the tune of 'J'ai une histoire à raconter' or 'En descendant la rue d'Alger'. It mocks the preface-manifesto, the 'directions for use', of Bourbaki's *Éléments*. The *chanson*, roughly translated, goes something like this:

> The directions for using this treatise (x 2)
> Are the height of simplicity (x 2)
> If there's something you still can't see,
> Never fear!
> Just think more abstractly
> And it will all become clear. (x 2)
> The alphabets of every nation (x 2)
> Will be used in explanations (x 2)
> For clarity's sake, we have
> Often enough
> Used the smallest font
> For the most important stuff. (x 2)
> The exercises are tantalizing (x 2)
> Their wording is so enticing (x 2)
> But don't bother trying to do
> A lot!
> We've heard two thirds of them
> Are false, or worse, are nonsense. (x 2)
> Our notations, as you'll see (x 2)
> Are as improved as they can be (x 2)
> According to the best of criteria
> Which is?
> That in the whole wide world
> No one can understand a single word. (x 2)

The order of the presentation (x 2)
Was the subject of long meditation (x 2)
We've put the secondary points
In front!
What's more, we've buried in corollaries
All the necessities: so you'll have to hunt. (x 2)[26]

Bourbaki were, therefore, already in the business of parodying Bourbaki (and doing so in verse) before Oulipo came on the scene. The Bourbaki movement was, at least in part, a series of experiments in genre: from their (admittedly minor) works of literary pastiche, through their parables and historiography, to the grand experiment of the *Éléments*, which turned the humble analysis textbook into the bearer of a utopian vision. Bourbaki's published writings and their archives show the tangled visions and discordant notes of their utopianism. Nonetheless, Bourbaki's nonformal structuralist image of mathematics gained traction both inside and outside the discipline of mathematics—evident not least in the formation of Oulipo itself.

8

The Oulipo—'Ouvroir de Littérature Potentielle', or 'Workshop of Potential Literature', had its first official meeting on 24 November 1960, summoned by Le Lionnais and the *quondam* surrealist writer, Raymond Queneau. Bourbaki's doctrine of potential formalization inspired and justified the Oulipo's project of potential literature. Queneau's manifesto defended Oulipo's playful use of mathematics to generate formal poetic constraints. After all, history shows us that ludic, impure uses of mathematics are often, in the end, vindicated:

> Let us remember that topology and the theory of numbers sprang in part from that which used to be called 'mathematical entertainments', 'recreational mathematics' . . . that the calculation of probabilities was at first nothing other than an anthology of 'diversions', as Bourbaki states in the 'Notice Historique' of the twenty-first fascicle on Integration. And likewise game theory, until von Neumann.[27]

---

[26] *La Tribu* 29, report on the 'Congrès de l'incarnation de l'Ane qui trotte', Celles-sur-Plaine, 19–26 October 1952, in *Archives de l'Association des Collaborateurs de Nicolas Bourbaki*.

[27] Raymond Queneau, 'Potential Literature', in Warren Motte, ed., *Oulipo: A Primer of Potential Literature*, London 1998, p. 51.

Oulipo draw on mathematics—combinatorial techniques, Boolean algebra and Bourbaki's axiomatic method, for example—in their literary practice. Their objective is to 'propose new "structures" to writers, mathematical in nature' or 'invent new artificial or mechanical procedures that will contribute to literary activity'. Queneau's manifesto went on to demonstrate a few Oulipean exercises: 'Redundancy in Mallarmé', 'The S + 7 Method' and 'Isomorphisms'.[28]

Bourbaki's structures were central to Le Lionnais's founding text for the group. 'Lipo: First Manifesto' begins as many manifestos do: by spoofing the genre's typically overblown rhetoric. 'Potential Literature' is announced as imminent, necessary and urgent: witness 'the impatience of the starving multitudes'. In Le Lionnais's re-casting, the Quarrel of the Ancients and the Moderns functions as a grandiose prehistory for the advent of Oulipo. The manifesto challenges its reader with absurd, overblown questions: 'Do you remember the polemic that accompanied the invention of language?'; 'And the creation of writing, and grammar, do you think that happened without a fight?'; 'Should humanity lie back and be satisfied to watch new thoughts make ancient verses?'[29]

9

A decade later, Le Lionnais's 'Second Manifesto' announced that it was time to broach 'the question of semantics'. Drawing on the rhetorical play of Bourbaki's 'The Architecture of Mathematics', he invoked an organic, biological register. Those sceptical of the Oulipo might ask:

> But can an artificial structure be viable? Does it have the slightest chance to take root in the cultural tissue of a society and to produce leaf, flower, and fruit? . . . One may compare this problem—*mutatis mutandis*—to that of the laboratory synthesis of living matter. That no one has ever succeeded in doing this doesn't prove a priori that it's impossible . . . Oulipo has preferred to put its shoulder to the wheel, recognizing furthermore that the

---

[28] Queneau, 'Potential Literature'. Redundancy: since the essence of Mallarmé's sonnets was concentrated in the last word of each line, the rest could be eliminated. S+7: take an existing text and replace every noun with the seventh noun after it in the dictionary. Isomorphism: replace words in a text with others that sound similar.
[29] François Le Lionnais, 'Lipo: First Manifesto' [1962] in *Oulipo: A Primer of Potential Literature*, pp. 26–9.

elaboration of artificial literary structures would seem to be infinitely less complicated and less difficult than the creation of life.[30]

If most artificial structures created by the Oulipo exist in a potential state, awaiting their cultural animation, some of those structures are discovered or uncovered in existing cultural forms: we stumble upon them in nature, so to speak. Le Lionnais's point recalls Bourbaki's remarks about mathematical structures and their relationship to empirical reality:

> From the axiomatic point of view mathematics appears on the whole as a reservoir of abstract *forms*—the mathematical structures; and it sometimes happens, without anyone really knowing why, that certain aspects of experimental reality model themselves after certain of these forms, as if by a sort of preadaptation.[31]

Indeed, it remains surprising—even astonishing—that the structures, equations and other paraphernalia that mathematicians invent for their own purposes so often turn out to be accurate models of natural processes or useful tools for understanding physical reality. Jean Piaget even considered the correspondence between Bourbaki's 'mother structures'—the algebraic structures, structures of order and topological structures—and the elementary 'operations' that children use as they begin to interact with the world.[32] What Bourbaki call 'preadaptation', Le Lionnais refers to as 'plagiarism by anticipation'. On occasion, he writes, the members of the Oulipo 'discover that a structure we believed to be entirely new had in fact already been discovered or invented in the past'. When this happens, Oulipo 'make it a point of honour to recognize such a state of things in qualifying the text in question as "plagiarism by anticipation"'.[33]

10

Many Oulipean texts are manifestos. Indeed, as the manifesto is a genre of potentiality—positioned between what has been done and what is to

---

[30] François Le Lionnais, 'Second Manifesto' [1973] in *Oulipo: A Primer of Potential Literature*, pp. 30–1.
[31] Bourbaki, 'The Architecture of Mathematics', p. 36.
[32] Jean Piaget, *Structuralism*, trans. Chaninah Maschler, London 1971, p. 28.
[33] Le Lionnais, 'Second Manifesto', p. 31.

be done—it is a particularly suitable vehicle for the group's 'Potential Literature'. The analogy between literature and mathematics is essential to the Oulipo. The group's members have included professional mathematicians like Roubaud himself, Claude Berge and Paul Braffort. Roubaud argues that for the members of Oulipo, the 'exhaustion' of traditional literary forms and rules 'is the starting point in the search for a *second foundation*, that of mathematics'. Oulipo want to replace rules with axiomatic constraints, and forms with Bourbakian structures. Where earlier literary and artistic avant-gardes—Vorticism, Futurism— developed and deployed diverse, often largely informal mathematical vernaculars, Oulipo sought to explicate and to codify their literary mathematics. Oulipo did not use mathematics simply as a legitimating discourse, as a code for their modernity, autonomy or aesthetic stance, nor merely as a source of metaphors; rather, for Roubaud, Queneau and their comrades, literature's affiliation with mathematics was and is an end in itself: 'Mathematics repairs the ruin of rules.'[34]

Yet, here we might pause and recall Adorno's criticism of such aesthetic affiliations with mathematics. For Adorno, although mathematics shares certain characteristics with art ('on the basis of its formalism, mathematics is itself aconceptual; its signs are not signs of something, and it no more formulates existential judgements than does art; its aesthetic quality has often been noted') attempts to directly equate aesthetic forms and mathematical forms are acts of self-deception and self-renunciation. Like Roubaud, Adorno saw the recourse to mathematics as motivated by the ruin of rules. Roubaud was content to look to mathematics for inspiration: for the axioms and structures through which to generate his 'potential literature'. Adorno, on the other hand, argued that mathematics could not repair the ruin of rules:

> Mathematization as a method for the immanent objectification of form is chimerical. Its insufficiency can perhaps be clarified by the fact that artists resort to it during historical periods when the traditional self-evidence of forms dissolves and no objective canon is available. At these moments the artist has recourse to mathematics; it unifies the level of subjective reason attained by the artist with the semblance of an objectivity founded on categories such as universality and necessity.[35]

---

[34] Jacques Roubaud, 'Mathematics in the Method of Raymond Queneau' in *Oulipo: A Primer of Potential Literature*, p. 93.
[35] Theodor Adorno, *Aesthetic Theory*, trans. Robert Hullot-Kentor, London 2009, p. 181.

For the artist to reach outside the domain of the aesthetic for a source of legitimacy is, however, only to further undermine art's claim to legitimacy. 'Rather than embodying the abiding lawfulness of being, its own claim to legitimacy', Adorno writes, 'the mathematical aspect of art despairingly strives to guarantee its possibility in a historical situation in which the objectivity of the conception of form is as requisite as it is inhibited by the level of consciousness'. Structures imported from mathematics might offer the 'semblance' of objectivity. Yet, Adorno argues, those structures and that objectivity crumble in the act of translation: 'the organization, the relation of elements to each other that constitutes form, does not originate in the specific structure and fails when confronted with the particular'.[36]

For the Oulipean Queneau, that crumbling, that failure, that patchy translation, was something to be embraced and represented. In 'The Foundations of Literature (after David Hilbert)', Queneau formulates an axiomatic system for literature.[37] The text is at once a tribute to Hilbert, a pastiche of Hilbert's axiomatic style and a critique of Hilbert. The first paragraph of *À la recherche du temps perdu*, Flaubert's sentence structure and chapter XCVIII of *Tristram Shandy* are variously sifted, filtered and warped as they are tested against the axioms lifted from Hilbert's *Foundations of Geometry* (1899). Queneau thus stages a confrontation between the axiomatic method and the particularities of literature, creating a manifesto that enacts, via its own internal logic, the impossibility of complete formalization.[38]

---

[36] Adorno, *Aesthetic Theory*, pp. 188–9.
[37] Hilbert had responded to Frege's objection to his axiomatic system by claiming: 'But it is surely obvious that every theory is only a scaffolding or schema of concepts together with their necessary relations to one another, and that the basic elements can be thought of in any way one likes. If in speaking of my points I think of some other system of things, e.g. the system: love, law, chimney-sweep . . . and then assume all my axioms as relations between these things, then my propositions, e.g. Pythagoras's theorem, are also valid for those things': David Hilbert to Gottlob Frege, 29 December 1899, excerpted by Frege, in Gottlob Frege, *Philosophical and Mathematical Correspondence*, Oxford 1980, Letter IV/4, p. 39.
[38] Raymond Queneau, 'The Foundations of Literature (after David Hilbert)' [1973], trans. Harry Mathews, in *Oulipo Laboratory: Texts from the Bibliothèque Oulipienne by Raymond Queneau, Italo Calvino, Paul Fournel, Jacques Jouet, Claude Berge & Harry Mathews*, London 1995, pp. 2–15.

'In these extraordinary portraits of exile Luke de Noronha illustrates through human experience how racism operates in Britain and beyond. This is what we mean when we say Black Lives Matter.'

Gary Younge, Professor of Sociology, University of Manchester

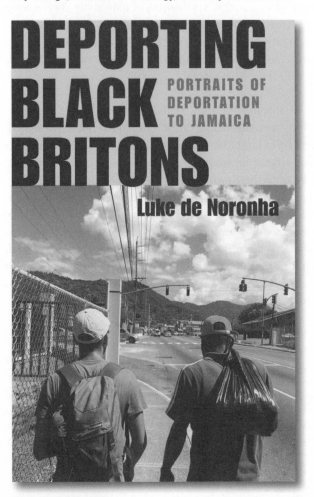

Manchester University Press

Publishing September 2020
£16.99

FRANCO MORETTI

THE ROADS TO ROME

Literary Studies, Hermeneutics, Quantification

W HAT RELATIONSHIP, between the quantitative literary history of the past twenty years, and the older hermeneutic tradition? Answers have typically been of two kinds: for many in the interpretive camp, the two approaches are incompatible, and the newer one has little or no critical value; for most quantitative researchers, they are instead perfectly compatible, and in fact complementary. Here, I will propose a third possibility, that will emerge step by step from a comparison of how the two strategies work. How they *work*, literally; in the conviction that, as Oleg Sobchuk and I have recently written, 'practices—what we learn to do by doing, by professional habit, and often without being fully aware of what we are doing—have frequently larger theoretical implications than theoretical statements themselves.'[1] In that article, 'practice' referred to the different ways of visualizing data; here, to the chain of interconnected decisions that shape an explanatory strategy. But the aim is the same: understanding what a research paradigm *does*, rather than what it declares it wants to do.

With a complication, however: since both the quantitative and—even more so—the hermeneutic approach are actually *many* approaches, often sharply at odds with each other (a Lacanian interpretation having nothing in common with a new historicist or an ecocritical one, and so on), in order to reduce the variables in play I will restrict myself to work I have personally taken part in. This is of course a questionable decision (and the exact opposite of 'Hidden in Plain Sight', which examined sixty-odd articles by over a hundred authors), which I am taking for two distinct reasons: first, because much of what follows will be quite critical, and I find it easier to criticize myself than others; second, because I've been repeatedly taken aback, in the past twenty years, by how different my work ended up being in the two registers. To some extent it *had* to be different of course (that's the whole point of using more than one method), but there was something slightly uncanny, in my drifting away from my own work. Maybe it's just a case of personal inconsistency; maybe, the sign of something larger, with an objective significance for the entire field.

I

Hermeneutics first. Nick Adams, the protagonist of Hemingway's short story 'Big Two-Hearted River' (1925), is about to go fishing:

> Nick took it from his hook book, sitting with the rod across his lap. He tested the knot and the spring of the rod by pulling the line taut. It was a good feeling. He was careful not to let the hook bite into his finger.
> He started down to the stream, holding his rod; the bottle of grass-hoppers hung from his neck by a thong tied in half hitches around the neck of the bottle. His landing net hung by a hook from his belt. Over his shoulder was a long flour sack tied at each corner into an ear. The cord went over his shoulder. The sack flapped against his legs.
> Nick felt awkward and professionally happy with all his equipment hanging from him. The grasshopper bottle swung against his chest. In his shirt the breast pockets bulged against him with his lunch and his fly book.[2]

First of all—does this passage even need an interpretation? Not really, if interpreting means dispelling the 'obscurity' of a text: here, everything seems perfectly clear. Is it, though? The idea 'that understanding occurs as a matter of course', wrote the founder of modern hermeneutics, is

[1] Franco Moretti and Oleg Sobchuk, 'Hidden in Plain Sight: Data Visualization in the Humanities', NLR 118, July–August 2019, pp. 86–115. 'Hidden in Plain Sight' and the current essay are part of a series of reflections on the quantitative study of culture that includes 'Operationalizing: Or, the Function of Measurement in Modern Literary Theory' (2013), 'Literature, Measured' (2016) and 'Patterns and Interpretation' (2017): the last three now collected in Moretti, ed., *Canon/Archive: Studies in Quantitative Formalism from the Stanford Literary Lab*, New York 2017, and 'Simulating Dramatic Networks', *Journal of World Literature*, Fall 2020.
[2] Ernest Hemingway, *The Nick Adams Stories*, New York 1981, p. 190. The analysis that follows condenses the more detailed account I have given in *Far Country: Scenes from American Culture*, New York and London 2019, pp. 49–65.

typical of the 'less rigorous practice' of interpretation; for its 'more rigorous' version it is however '*mis*understanding [that] occurs as a matter of course, and understanding must therefore be willed and sought at every point'.[3]

Willed at every point . . . Let's start with this, then: that this handful of sentences include *twenty-five* prepositional phrases (those introduced by a preposition: 'from his hook book', 'across his lap' and so on).[4] Twenty-five in 149 words: a lot. But they are there, because they are doing something which is essential to the story: gluing together all sorts of disparate elements. 'The *bottle* of *grasshoppers* hung from his *neck* by a *thong* tied in half *hitches* around the *neck* of the *bottle*.' A Swiss army knife: an incredibly compressed and well-organized world. A world *of things*:

> With the *ax* he slit off a bright *slab* of *pine* from one of the *stumps* and split it into *pegs* for the *tent*. He wanted them long and solid to hold the ground . . . He pegged the sides out taut and drove the pegs deep, hitting them down into the ground with the flat of the ax until the rope loops were buried and the canvas was drum tight.[5]

A world of things, but not only: Nick wants pegs '*for* the tent'; they are 'long and solid *to* hold the ground', and he hits them '*until* the rope loops were buried'. It's all so *purposeful*: done, in order to do something else. 'Know how', Gilbert Ryle called these chains of silent interlinked movements. 'Nick tied the rope . . . *and* pulled the tent up . . . *and* tied it to the

---

[3] The passages come from Friedrich Schleiermacher's programmatic 'Compendium' of 1819: see Heinz Kimmerle, ed., *Hermeneutics: The Handwritten Manuscripts*, Missoula MT 1977, pp. 109, 110. 'Obscurity', Peter Szondi rightly observed, is for Schleiermacher 'hardly the only occasion for interpretation': *Introduction to Literary Hermeneutics*, Cambridge 1995 [1975], p. 27.
[4] Here they are, in italics: 'Nick took it *from his hook book*, sitting *with the rod* / *across his lap*. He tested the knot and the spring *of the rod* by pulling the line taut. It was a good feeling. He was careful not to let the hook bite *into his finger*. He started *down to the stream*, holding his rod, the bottle *of grasshoppers* hung *from his neck* / *by a thong* tied *in half hitches* / *around the neck* / *of the bottle*. His landing net hung *by a hook* / *from his belt*. / *Over his shoulder* was a long flour sack tied *at each corner* / *into an ear*. The cord went *over his shoulder*. The sack flapped *against his legs*. Nick felt awkward and professionally happy *with all his equipment* hanging *from him*. The grasshopper bottle swung *against his chest*. *In his shirt* the breast pockets bulged *against him* / *with his lunch and his fly book*.'
[5] Hemingway, *The Nick Adams Stories*, p. 183.

other pine.' Always calm, always efficient. But: this is a story. Isn't calm the opposite of what a story needs?

It is. But Hemingway was writing within a very special historical context. We usually turn to stories because our life is not eventful enough; but what if the key experience of an entire generation has been the Great War? Much *too* eventful: and so, the desire for a different kind of narrative arises, where calm has a role to play. War literature, observed Eric Leed, is about 'men who, as a rule, had little or no control over the events which threatened their lives.'[6] No control: that is the key. Hemingway's style is *all about control*: of space, time, gestures, words. 'Nick felt awkward and professionally happy with all his equipment hanging from him': this is the snapshot of a young soldier—before the war. And the same goes for his march through the woods, his reconnaissance, his tent, his camp—he even eats canned food, on his trip. While not quite 'playing' at war, Nick is certainly *replaying* it. Rewriting it. Life in the trenches had alternated between tedium and terror; nothing for days, then apocalypse. Hemingway's prose is never boring, and never frightening; clean and cautious, it's the perfect style for *convalescence* (three years later, the central episode—and happiest—of his first great success, *A Farewell to Arms*). This is war literature in the sense that it wants to *recover* from the war: to resolve the dissonance of historical experience, to adapt Lukács's metaphor in *Theory of the Novel*. But on this, more later.

2

From a few sentences of a single short story, to the most evident novelty of the quantitative approach: the expansion of literary history well beyond a small canon of great works. Time was, a theorist would choose one text—*Don Quixote, Robinson Crusoe, The Idiot*—and erect upon it a whole theory of the novel. 'Type thinking', Ernst Mayr has called it: '*Tristram Shandy* is *the most typical novel* in all of world literature', as Shklovsky wrote in *Theory of Prose*.[7] In front of the swarm of nineteenth-century British novels of Figure 1, though, type thinking is useless: here, one must account for an entire 'population' of novels. Not a very large one, in this case—1,117, to be exact—but still irreducible to a single text.

[6] Eric J. Leed, *No Man's Land*, Cambridge 1981, p. 33.
[7] Viktor Shklovsky, *Theory of Prose*, 1925–29, Elmwood Park IL 1991, p. 170.

FIGURE I

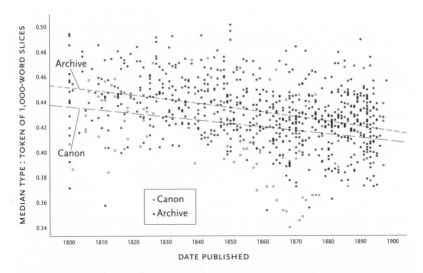

Source: Mark Algee-Hewitt, Sarah Allison, Marissa Gemma, Ryan Heuser, Franco Moretti and Hannah Walser, 'Canon/Archive: Large-Scale Dynamics in the Literary Field', Stanford Literary Lab, Pamphlet II, January 2016.[8]

The text: this is where the discord between old and new is at its sharp-est. It used to be *the* object of literary study; here, it's a dot. It has been *made* to be a dot. Downsized, just like 'events' had been, during the great quantitative turn of seventy years ago. Events used to be as cen-tral to historiography as texts to literary study, and for the same reason: because of their uniqueness. 'Historians resembled collectors', wrote Krzysztof Pomian in his retrospective on the *Annales*, 'gather[ing] only rare and curious objects, and ignoring whatever looked banal, everyday, normal . . .' Once events started to be studied 'as elements of a series', however, uniqueness lost its significance, and individual events ended up being 'relegated to the periphery of history, or disregarded altogether'.[9] A history that disregards events: this is the quantitative turn. A history of art without names, Wölfflin once wrote. A history of literature without texts.

---

[8] The study has now been collected in *Canon/Archive*. Here, too, what follows is only a very abbreviated summary of the original.

[9] Krzysztof Pomian, 'L'histoire des structures', in Jacques Le Goff, Roger Chartier and Jacques Revel, eds, *La Nouvelle Histoire*, Paris 1978, pp. 536, 543–4.

Without texts—in the sense that *there are too many of them,* of course, and they can therefore no longer be studied as individual cases: as is indeed the case for the 250 canonical and 850 forgotten novels of Figure 1. We wanted to know whether linguistic richness contributed to a novel's survival or oblivion, so all texts were sliced into 1,000-word segments, and their type–token ratio was calculated.[10] And it turned out that the segment with the highest score belonged to Edward Hawker's *Arthur Montague, or an Only Son at Sea* (1850), and that with the lowest one to George Eliot's *Adam Bede* (1859).[11]

That a novel none of us had heard of should have so much more lexical variety than a canonical one like Eliot's was the opposite of what we expected, so we of course read those two segments quite carefully. Hawker's was a description: which makes sense, because descriptions require details, and details increase lexical variety. Eliot's was completely different: a young woman, confessing to having abandoned her child to die, and repeating the same words over and over again (thus uttering the most redundant passage of the entire century), as if she were chained— 'but I couldn't go away'—to that scene of trauma. At this point we read the other segments that clustered around them at the two ends of the

---

[10] Type–token ratio is a standard measure of lexical variety, that expresses the relationship between the number of *different* words used (types), and the number of *actual* words used (tokens). 'Good morning, my good friend' has four types and five tokens, hence a type–token ratio of 4/5, or 0.8; 'Good morning, Jim, good morning' has also five tokens, but only three types, hence a type–token ratio of 3/5, or 0.6.

[11] Here are two sections of those extreme segments, where the hash sign indicates a word that had already appeared in the segment, and the asterisk a word that did not belong to the initial 'dictionary' of novelistic English (about 230,000 words) created by Ryan Heuser, who wrote the program for this part of the experiment.

Arthur Montague: 'then cut through some acres of refreshing greensward, studded with the oak, walnut, and hawthorn, ascended a knoll, skirted an expansive sheet of# water; afterwards entering an# avenue of# noble elms, always tenanted* by a# countless host of# cawing* rooks, whose clamorous conclaves* interrupted the# stillness that reigned around, and# whose# visits to adjacent corn-fields* of# inviting aspect raised the# ire and# outcry of# the# yelling urchins employed to# guard them from depredation.'

Adam Bede: 'And# I# made haste out# of# the# wood#, but# I# could# hear it# crying# all# the# while#; and# when# I# got# out# into# the# fields#, it# was# as# if# I# was# held fast#-- I# could# n't go# away#, for# all# I# wanted so# to# go#. And# I# sat# against# the# haystack# to# watch if# anybody# 'ud come#: I# was# very# hungry, and# I#'d only a# bit of# bread# left; but# I# could# n't go# away#.'

spectrum (from *Ennui, Tales of a Briefless Barrister, Marius the Epicurean, Lady Laura*, and dozens of others), and felt we could generalize: high type–token ratio was consistently associated with the prose of the novel-istic narrator: written, analytical, impersonal, and almost atemporal; low type–token ratio, to the voice of novelistic characters at specific moments of high emotional intensity.

This is what reading texts as elements of a series is like: we no longer wanted to go from the segment of *Adam Bede* to the representation of infanticide and its role in Victorian culture (as I had done with Hemingway); we wanted to go from that segment *to many other segments*, in order to construct a set of conceptual pairs—narrator/character, written/spoken, analytical/emotional and so on—that would help chart the space of narrative possibilities. Ideally, the *whole* space. Not easy, as we found out—we tried to make sense of the segments lying at the centre of the distribution, and failed[12]—but the direction was clear: we were no longer studying texts, but *series* of texts. Different.

3

Twelve sentences; 1,100 novels. The interpretation of a text; the meas-urement of a corpus. And the question returns: what relationship, between them?

First of all, they are both perfectly valid forms of knowledge: on this, the broadsides from the interpretive camp are entirely groundless. Both valid—and with a moment of overlap, too. In the midst of measurement, there had been interpretation: we had taken Hawker's 'acres of refresh-ing greensward, studded with oak, walnut, and hawthorn', and turned it into—which is to say: interpreted it as—'impersonal analytical prose of the novelistic narrator'. Conversely, the interpretation of 'Big Two-Hearted River' had been triggered by a (very elementary) form of measurement: it was because prepositional phrases were so insanely frequent that I had

---

[12] We failed, because extreme cases like *Arthur Montague* and *Adam Bede* possess an epistemological clarity that average ones lack. For a similar interplay of the extreme and the average, where the latter was analyzed a little more successfully, see Mark Algee-Hewitt, Ryan Heuser and Franco Moretti, 'On Paragraphs: Scale, Themes, and Narrative Form', now in *Canon/Archive*.

noticed them, and 'willed my understanding', as Schleiermacher had put it. To some extent, each method had relied on the other, thus evoking the 'oscillation' advocated by various quantitative researchers: a type of work 'moving back and forth between close and distant forms of reading in order to approach an imaginary conceptual centre'.[13]

Moving back and forth . . . Was that what had happened? I had counted up to twenty-five while working on Hemingway; and yet, this kinder-garten feat had felt like all the measurement I needed. Same for *Adam Bede*: Hetty's confession was an extraordinary passage for interpretation to work on; we did almost nothing with it, and yet, again, it felt like all the interpretation we needed. And it felt that way, because both studies entailed a very clear hierarchy between the two methods: measurement was the means and interpretation the end in Hemingway's case, and vice versa with the 1,100 novels. With 'Big Two-Hearted River', the aim was understanding how a story about trout-fishing could be so significant (its popularity in American universities is legendary) even for readers who presumably couldn't care less about trout; there had to be *something more* than just fishing in it, and when I saw all those prepositional phrases I thought they might help me discover that 'something'. But I was focus-ing on the *grammar* of the phrases: that there were twenty-five of them, or eighteen, or thirty, made no difference at all.[14] Conversely with *Adam Bede*; we were measuring type–token ratio, and those obnoxious hash tags were the perfect sign of our priorities: they showed repetitions right away, which was what we wanted, and if they also turned reading into

---

[13] Andrew Piper, 'Novel Devotions: Conversional Reading, Computational Modeling and the Modern Novel', *New Literary History*, vol. 46, no. 1, Winter 2015, pp. 67–8. Similarly, Hoyt Long and Richard Jean So have urged 'a method of reading that oscillates or pivots between human and machine interpretation, each providing feedback to the other in the critic's effort to extract meaning from texts': 'Literary Pattern Recognition: Modernism between Close Reading and Machine Learning', *Critical Inquiry*, vol. 42, no. 2, Winter 2016, p. 267.

[14] Better: there had to be enough of them to become visible, as is always the case in stylistic criticism; exactly how many counted as 'enough' could however remain vague. See, by contrast, the precision with which Sarah Allison and Marissa Gemma established the link between the register of conversation in the *Longman Grammar of Spoken and Written English* (mean type–token ratio of 30 per cent), and the 500 lowest-ranked segments of our corpus, where type–token ratio oscillated between 27 and 33 per cent: *Canon/Archive*, p. 283. In their reflections, the pathos of research was inextricable from an accuracy that is unimaginable in the herme-neutic tradition.

a nightmare—well, reading was not the point here. Not for nothing, the next steps we took were a series of correlations of type–token ratio with abstract grammatical categories that got rid of text, reading and interpretation altogether.[15]

I will describe how research actually works, I said at the start, and now you see what I meant: it is in the concrete decisions that at the time seem purely 'tactical'—inserting hash tags, not keeping an exact count of prepositions, turning towards a historical event, measuring another variable of the corpus—it is in these apparently minor choices that 'strategic' research priorities take form. Priorities, and exclusions: there had been a moment of overlap between the two methods, yes—and then it passed. More precisely, it was dropped. As the work proceeded, interpretation became ever more interpretive, and quantification more quantitative. Once the critical pendulum had started swinging in one direction, it never came back. There was no oscillation here, and no conceptual centre.

But perhaps there could be? Those studies had a one-sided aim from the start, which is why they subordinated one method to the other. Couldn't one design a study in which they had exactly the same weight?

I know of no such study; but in principle it's certainly possible. We can easily interpret Eliot's sentences as thoroughly as Hemingway's, or measure the exact frequency of prepositional phrases in all American short stories of the 1920s. Nothing prevents the two methods from working next to each other. Can they also work *together*? This is the point. Quantification can provide new objects for hermeneutic activity, and interpretations lend themselves to quantitative testing: this we know.[16] What is at stake here, though, is different: it's *the categories* of literary analysis. Can quantitative and hermeneutic categories lock onto each other, so as to *conceptually unify* the two approaches? Aby Warburg's *Pathosformel*, Jakobson's rethinking of poetry and prose in the light of aphasia, Bourdieu's 'field', Schwarz's 'debt' as a key to literary history: plenty of bold conceptual bridges have been launched between distant

---

[15] See figures 9.19–21 in *Canon/Archive*, pp. 283–5.
[16] On this, see my 'Patterns and Interpretation', now in *Canon/Archive*, Sarah Allison's *Reductive Reading: A Syntax of Victorian Moralizing*, Baltimore 2018, especially pp. 19ff, and Ted Underwood's *Distant Horizons*, Chicago 2019, *passim*.

disciplines in the past. Why is it so difficult this time? None of us is a Warburg or a Jakobson: granted. Is that the only reason?

4

Certain features, writes Georges Canguilhem in his great study of nineteenth-century medical epistemology,

> are termed normal insofar as they designate average characteristics, which are most frequently practically observable. But they are also termed normal because they enter ideally into that normative activity called therapeutics . . . the normal state designates both the habitual state of the organs, and their ideal.[17]

The normal as frequent-habitual-average, and the normal as ideal-normative: one signifier, and two distinct concepts. What relationship, between quantitative and hermeneutic categories? The same: the former focus on the frequent-average aspects of literature, and the latter on its normative side. Normative, in the sense Panofsky had in mind when he spoke of art as 'an objectifying conflict, aiming at definitive results, between a forming power and a material to be overcome'.[18] *Bewältigen*: mastering, remoulding, overcoming historical materials by applying the force—*Kraft*—of aesthetic form. This is the normative side of art and literature: one takes what is there, and turns it into something else. And this is also what interpretation works on, or, better, works *against*. Against, because interpretation is always a struggle with the text: it takes those 'definitive results', and tries as hard as possible *to undo the work of form*: to move backwards from the text as it is, through its techniques, to the world around it, and the 'dissonance' that was being addressed. In this sense, interpretation is an understanding of literature that is always tempted to go *beyond literature*: like the essayists described in *Soul and Form*, who pretend to be only discussing books, though they are actually 'always talking about the ultimate questions of life'.

Not that interpretation always goes that far. But it can: whereas the quantitative approach cannot. With the single text that is the typical object of

---

[17] Georges Canguilhem, *The Normal and the Pathological*, New York 1989, pp. 122–3, 126.
[18] Erwin Panofsky, 'Der Begriff des Kunstwollens', *Zeitschrift für Ästhetik und Allgemeine Kunstwissenschaft*, vol. 14, 1920, p. 339.

hermeneutics, reverse-engineering may suggest which of the countless aspects of historical reality we should focus on; morphology, acting as the catalyst for historical intuition.[19] With hundreds of texts—let alone more—this becomes impossible, and the 'vertical' link between the text and the world is replaced by a 'horizontal' one among texts that are all on the same plane. Hemingway's sentences had led me to the war; Eliot's segment, *to other segments*. It's striking, how literature-bound the quantitative approach has turned out to be.

Quantification, imprisoned among books. A flaw? Not at all. If one dimension is lost, in the shift from hermeneutics to quantification, one dimension is gained: we still know almost nothing about how literary systems function, and that's exactly what the logic of measurement shifts our gaze towards. In this sense, the cluster of morphological features emerging from those 1,100 dots had been a small but real step in the right direction: fixing a few stars in the infinite night sky of the literary field. A task, this one, that the hermeneutic tradition, with all its creativity, has never been curious about.

5

What relationship, between hermeneutics and quantification? When I started studying for this essay, I didn't know what the answer would be. Having worked for years now with one method and now with the other—but never together—I had been fantasizing about a book to come that might reach a synthesis of sorts: an 'emergent' theory of literature, where the meeting of micro and macro would be more than the sum of its parts. Then I started describing what I had actually done, and the fantasy evaporated: the brief overlap between the two practices, or the lexical proximity of the normative and the frequent, were too weak a foundation for any genuine, long-term synthesis.

---

[19] The list of major phenomena (let alone minor ones) that could count as 'the world' for any work of literature is virtually infinite. For an American in Europe in the 1920s, it would indeed have included the trenches of World War I, but also a socialist revolution, cars and aeroplanes, a decade of unprecedented sexual freedom, civil wars, rationalist architecture, the radio, incredible experiments in painting and music, the beginning of hyper-inflation . . . A single form usually reacts to only a few of these phenomena, which interpretation may succeed in isolating; with a large corpus, however, formal mechanisms multiply in every direction, and the threads that lead from the works to the world become hopelessly tangled.

Perhaps, I should have known it all along. Interpretation *transforms* all it touches: 'this, means that'. Quantification takes pride in an utter respect for its data. The impulses are antithetical. Dionysus, Apollo. Think of how they relate to form. Interpretation moves *between form and the world*, pursuing the broad historical significance of literary works; quantification moves *between form and form*, trying to define the coordinates of an as yet uncharted literary atlas. Here, form is *a force*: an 'overcoming' of historical materials which must be met with suspicion, countered and ultimately unmasked. There, it is *a product*, to be measured with a cool head, and placed within a many-sided system of relations. Interpretation leads towards history, and is animated by the pathos of struggle; quantification towards morphology, animated by the pathos of discovery. Great passions, both of them. But too exclusive to join forces towards a common goal. They can certainly—let me repeat it—work one next to the other, offering new objects of study to their respective fields. But they cannot *intervene in each other's work*. Night and day; one begins, the other vanishes. Always chasing each other, and never becoming one.

For some, this is plenty; for others, maybe even too much; for me . . . not what I'd been hoping for. But there is a logic to critical work, and we should try to understand it—to understand *what we're actually doing when we're studying literature*—rather than conjuring up a synthesis no one has ever seen. In the end, there is nothing wrong in studying a complicated object like literature in two entirely independent ways. Or at least: this is my view of the matter. Needless to say, I may be wrong, and someone might find a good synthesis—tomorrow. Then, things change. Until then, as Arnold Schönberg once said, the middle road remains the only one that does not lead to Rome.

K. S. Komireddi, *Malevolent Republic: A Short History of the New India*
Hurst: London 2019, £20, hardback
259 pp, 978 1 787 38005 9

ALPA SHAH

EXPLAINING MODI

If the opinion polls are right, India's Narendra Modi is currently the world's most popular leader. His approval rating was over 80 per cent at the height of the pandemic in April and May this year, with Johnson, Trudeau and López Obrador in the low 60s, while Trump, Macron and Abe all failed to reach 50 per cent. The 2019 elections gave him a second term with a commanding majority of Lok Sabha seats. At the same time, Modi's record towards his country's minorities—imposing martial law on Kashmir, excluding Muslims from the 2019 Citizenship (Amendment) Act, quietly tolerating an epidemic of lynchings, burnings and beatings of Muslims and Dalits—has been qualitatively more brutal than that of Bolsonaro or Trump. How should we account for the Modi phenomenon? The starting point of Kapil Komireddi's *Malevolent Republic* is that Modi should not be seen as an aberration: that would be 'a self-comforting lie'. Instead, Komireddi—a freelance journalist from Hyderabad, now based in the West—offers three reasons for his rise.

First, *Malevolent Republic* points to decades of Congress Party failings—above all, the corruption, nepotism, authoritarianism and greed of its ruling family. Although Nehru and Gandhi are absolved, from the 1960s the party became 'a sump for Nehru's parasitical progeny to luxuriate in'. The first half of the book is a ruthless chronological accounting of Congress misdeeds, as leader after leader is excoriated in the run up to Modi: 'Erosion', 'Surrender', 'Decadence', 'Dissolution', run the chapter headings. Nehru's daughter

Indira displayed 'despotic impulses', using Congress 'as a laboratory to test her will', while her son Sanjay lacked even a 'residue of democratic inclination', as exemplified in the slum-clearance and sterilization campaigns he ran during the 1975–77 period of Emergency Rule. Millions of people lost their homes as entire districts were bulldozed in Sanjay's 'beautification' projects, while millions of poor and vulnerable men were dragged under the knife to meet his 'family-planning' targets. Dissenters, defenders of democratic rights, trade unionists, socialists, were imprisoned without charge, the press was heavily censored, foreign journalists expelled and Sanjay glorified by the media.

After the blowback from Indira's military assault on the Sikhs' Golden Temple—she was assassinated in 1984 by her own Sikh bodyguards—her other son, Rajiv, initiated his reign with a pogrom orchestrated by local Congress leaders. Three thousand Sikhs were killed in Delhi, police even disarming Sikh areas before the mob marched in—setting a precedent, Komireddi notes, for the slaughter of Muslims that took place in Gujarat under Modi in 2002. It was Rajiv who ordered that the gates of Ayodhya be opened, allowing Hindu nationalists to lay the foundations for a future temple inside the Babri Mosque. When Muslim leaders protested, Rajiv appeased them by banning Salman Rushdie's *Satanic Verses*, having already sabotaged Muslim women's rights in the Shah Bano case. After Rajiv's assassination—blowback again: having sent Indian troops into Sri Lanka, he was killed by a Tamil suicide bomber—the new Congress leader, Narasimha Rao, cultivated ties with the BJP, staying silent as the Babri Mosque was destroyed. The Congress Finance Minister, Manmohan Singh, is denounced by Komireddi as a 'subcontinental Pinochet' for his counter-insurgency against the Naxalites and his harsh neoliberal measures, cutting subsidies and handing land over to foreign corporations. Rapid economic growth was accompanied by rising inequality. Demoralized by decades of Congress betrayals, unshackled by Rao and Singh's neoliberal reforms from Nehruvian ideals of self-restraint, the expanding Hindu middle class was ready to see in the violence of Ayodhya and its follow-ups 'a self-empowering, even redemptive, message'.

Second, *Malevolent Republic* turns upon India's 'secular historians' and public intellectuals. Romila Thapar, author of the renowned Penguin *History of India, Volume One* and many other works on early Indian history, is a particular target. According to Komireddi, these scholars' 'well-intentioned sanitization of the past' failed to supply an adequate account of the Persian and Moghul imperial invasions of northern India and the centuries of Muslim rule. In the first decades after Independence, he argues, these intellectuals squandered the chance to provide (Hindu) Indians with a forthright narrative of their 'ravaged' heritage—the great mosques built from shattered temple fragments—that could have reconciled them to their 'harrowing past' and allowed a mature detachment from it. Instead, Thapar and her colleagues 'papered over the gruesome deeds of the invaders with nice-nellyisms', preferring to dwell on their cultural achievements. School textbooks presented an idyllic picture of medieval India in which Muslims and Hindus coexisted in harmony, shattered only by the arrival of the British. But the Muslim encounter left a 'deep wound', Komireddi argues. The euphemization of Moghul rule by Thapar and her colleagues had 'infantilized Indians', rendering them susceptible to 'the piffle of Hindu nationalists' who seized the chance to 'weaponize history', portraying Muslims as insensitive to innocent Hindus' wounded feelings. This, according to *Malevolent Republic*, provides the second precondition for Modi's rise: 'The confusion of a country that deferred the task of dealing sincerely with its wounded past was ripe for exploitation'.

Third, Komireddi argues, big-business backing—from the Tatas to the Ambani brothers—and praise from such eminent scholars as Columbia's Jagdish Bhagwati or Gurcharan Das, Harvard-educated author of *India Unbound*, were crucial to the BJP's success. 'Intellectuals and industrialists' polished Modi's image as a 'technocratic modernizer', celebrated his 'vision' and ability to get things done. And India's 'shameless elites were easily co-opted to pimp for him, asking only for a commitment to the market in return'. Foreign investors, diplomats and politicians made the pilgrimage to Modi's capital in Gandhinagar for his trade fairs when he was chief minister of Gujarat, from 2001–14. Although Gujarat's growth was accompanied by low social mobility, it was widely presented as the development model of India, with perfect roads, electricity and clean water. Support from the West was equally fulsome, and the 2002 Gujarati massacre soon forgotten. Before the 2014 election, *Time* magazine listed Modi as one of the world's most influential leaders, Cameron put on an honour guard for him, Hollande organized a boat ride on the Seine, Obama offered flattery. Hence 'there wasn't a shadow of resistance as Narendra Modi stormed Delhi in the summer of 2014'.

The second half of *Malevolent Republic* covers Modi's record in office. A series of short thematic chapters explore the Modi personality cult (3D holographic projectors beaming his image into villages without electricity); the monstrously bungled 'de-monetization' policy; the rise of cow vigilantes and escalation of anti-Muslim violence; and the assertion of BJP influence across India's institutions, from the Reserve Bank of India to the universities and Supreme Court. The treatment here is more journalistic; much of the material will be familiar to readers of the international press. On Kashmir and on foreign policy, however, Komireddi emerges as a hard-line hawk. He commends Modi for cutting an 'imposing figure on the world stage', 'confidently projecting Delhi as a rival to Beijing' and 'translating his muscular attitude into action' by sending troops into Bhutan in 2017 to block a Chinese road-building project. He then dismisses him for being insufficiently tough when the Bhutan invasion 'collapsed into a desperate face-saving exercise' after Washington declined to send reinforcements. Above all, the book is suffused with hostility to Pakistan—a 'monument to majoritarian bigotry', gripped by 'neurotic nationalism', ruled by 'vultures'. Alone of the many leaders Komireddi discusses, Bhutto, Pakistan's prime minister in the 1970s, is disparagingly referred to as 'Zulfi' at every point.

What explains *Malevolent Republic*'s hyper-aggressive regional-policy line, apparently out-Modi-ing Modi? The answer may lie in Komireddi's *cursus* as a journalist. He owes a major debt, he explains, to the mentorship of David Frum, the neoconservative Canadian-American publicist best known for coining the 'axis of evil' slogan for Bush's 2002 State of the Union address. In 2009, Frum recruited Komireddi, fresh out of US law school and without a clear idea of what he wanted to do, and funded him to tour Pakistan to produce a 10-part series for the Frum Forum website, under the title 'Pakistan: Anatomy of a Failed State'. Frum's editorializing sets the tone: 'India's success at forging a nationality out of its diversity stood as a towering repudiation of the very idea of Pakistan'—'Pakistan could not succeed unless India failed.' Or again: 'The terrorism with which we contend has its origins in Pakistan as much as in the Arab Middle East. Our friend Kapil Komireddi has returned from traveling inside Pakistan . . .' Also in 2009, Komireddi—presumably with Frum's help—published a 'stand up to China' piece in *Foreign Policy* ('Time for India to play hardball with China') and a *Guardian* opinion column on Kashmir: 'Over 60 arduous years, India has integrated radically diverse regions under the banner of a pluralistic nationalism. Its failure to achieve that in Kashmir is largely due to Pakistan.'

It would be wrong to consider Komireddi a neo-con, as *Malevolent Republic* makes clear. He warns Modi not to turn India into 'a frontline state in someone else's strategy to contain China' and attacks 'well-heeled Indians, besotted with visions of high status crafted in Washington', who dreamed of sending troops to Iraq in 2003. He mocks those members of India's elite who can be flattered into envisaging a global-power role that the country's internal realities—lack of clean water or sanitation—do not justify. In a 2015 *Guardian* piece, he saluted Corbyn for his anti-colonial track record; not something Frum would do. But Komireddi's partisan geopolitical formation—anti-Pakistan, above all, but also anti-China—is a constant drum-beat in the book. Commissioned by his London publisher as an overview of 'the new India' under Modi, Komireddi describes how *Malevolent Republic* turned into something else: a polemic, pitched at the level of a tirade.

How should one evaluate this strange, often self-contradictory book? Komireddi's explanation for Modi's rise is a welcome departure from the standard Western-liberal line which attributes the advance of populist 'strongmen' to a skilled and cynical manipulation of lower-class prejudice, mobilizing the resentments of neoliberalism's 'left-behinds' against blameless liberal elites. He rightly castigates the Congress record—and India's mainstream media—and spells out how much support Modi had from Obama, Cameron, Hollande. At the same time, his account is warped by its Indian-nationalist—or, perhaps, Frummist—detestation for Pakistan, which requires him to attribute sole responsibility for Partition to Jinnah, while absolving Nehruvian India of any blame. The conduct of Pakistan's ruling bloc offers plenty of easy targets, and readers can't be reminded often enough of the 1971 butchery in East Pakistan that midwifed the birth of Bangladesh. Komireddi has good grounds for saying that, on the basis of its treatment of its own citizens, the Pakistan government can barely lay claim to be a protector of Muslims in the region. However, a genuinely 'secular' critic would apply the same level of scrutiny to both sides.

Instead, Komireddi's Manichaean hostility towards Pakistan necessitates a systematic whitewashing of Nehru (*Malevolent Republic* has little to say about Gandhi). Nehru is portrayed racing to scenes of communal clashes without regard for his personal safety, threatening Hindu mobs plotting to massacre Muslims and striving to be 'a model of democratic leadership'. Yet while accusing Indian secular historians of airbrushing the military conquests of several hundred years ago, Komireddi does the same for the blood spilled within living memory on Nehru's orders. In his account, Nehru bears no responsibility for the slaughter of perhaps 40,000 Muslims by the troops he dispatched to put down the left-led uprising against the Nizam of Hyderabad in 1947 (nor for the suppression of the report into the massacre). Nehru's order for the military seizure of Kashmir in 1947—Indian forces were airlifted to Srinagar and took possession of most of the province—didn't go far enough for Komireddi, who thinks India should have taken the entire territory. *Malevolent Republic* also suggests that China initiated the 1962 border war against an over-tolerant Nehru—who, in fact, provoked it.

Ultimately, Komireddi's case against Modi doesn't manage to transcend a nationalism adjacent to the one Modi embodies, for his golden age of 'Indian secularism' is above all needed to provide ideological cover for Indian control over its Muslim-majority state; as he confesses, 'an India that has ceased to be secular has absolutely no claim to Kashmir.' Yet the realities behind an 'Idea of India' based on multicultural unity and impartial secularity go entirely unexamined. While attacking 'majoritarian bigotry' in Pakistan, Komireddi avoids any account of the Hindu pietism that was suffused into the national movement from the beginning by

Gandhi, majoritarian on a far larger scale. The same one-sidedness is apparent in his approach to Hinduism: how 'tolerant' can a religion be that is founded on untouchability, that maintains the deep entrenchments of caste and its rigid strictures against inter-caste marriage, and upholds the violence of deep-seated patriarchy? Such questions go unasked in *Malevolent Republic*, where Hindu violence appears only as an aberration created by corrupt Congress politicians.

Preoccupied by his anti-Pakistan polemic, Komireddi shows little interest in the broader debates in India about the extent to which the Modi regime represents a rupture with the past—work by Aijaz Ahmad, Angana Chatterji, Achin Vanaik, Ashutosh Varshney, John Hariss, Paul Brass and others; indeed, most of his references are to Western media sources. He pays no attention to the changing class/caste politics underway in India—where, ironically, as Christophe Jaffrelot and Thomas Blom Hansen have discussed, the rise of Modi has entailed a broader level of political participation among lower castes, entering spheres that were once the class privilege of a small elite. Significantly, Komireddi has almost nothing to say about the BJP or the broader Sangh Parivar 'family', whose cadres underpin Modi's position. For decades, the Sangh has been doing patient organizational work across the country and abroad (the excellent scholarship by Peggy Froerer, Tariq Thachil and others on this belies Komireddi's great-man view of history).

The Sangh has nurtured volunteers and foot soldiers from multiple sections of society. In addition to the RSS, there is the World Hindu Council (VHP)—set up to forge a corporate Hindu identity and unite all Hindu sects in opposition to Islam—which generates vast funds for Modi's campaigns, as well as the many affiliates of the RSS: trade unions, peasant organizations, women's wing, student wing and hundreds of NGOs. These organizations have spent years embedding themselves in Indian society, through both the provision of welfare services—schools, health clinics, community centres— and what Paul Brass has called institutionalized riot systems. In addition to their work in the Hindu heartlands, the *pracharaks* (propagators) have been riding out on motorbikes to remote Adivasi villages, converting local socioeconomic tensions into communal conflict. They have used sports, leisure and a vast network of private schools to create a new sense of discipline and a communalized vision of cultural heritage and history that amounts to a transformation of the idea of the Hindu-self—a process that it is crucial for any counter-hegemonic programme to understand. Though in some respects the ferocity of *Malevolent Republic*'s critique, both of India under Modi and of the Congress era which paved the way for it, is much needed right now, those seeking what 'a history of the new India' appears to promise—a multi-faceted account of the Sangh Parivar's assertion of hegemony over this vast country—will have to look elsewhere.

Yoram Hazony, *The Virtue of Nationalism*
Basic Books: New York 2018, £17.99, hardback
304 pp, 978 1 5416 4538 7

Nᴉᴄᴋ Bᴜʀɴs

CHOSEN NATIONS

Yoram Hazony presents himself as the leader of a rejuvenated American
nationalist right: an impresario, organizing conferences in the United States
and Europe; and as a theorist, setting out a programme for the new movement in his latest book, *The Virtue of Nationalism*. The book may be read on
two levels, on the one hand for its argument and on the other as an indicator
of the coalitions and fissures on the contemporary American right. The son
of an Israeli nuclear physicist, Yoram was raised in the United States. As an
undergraduate at Princeton in the mid-eighties, he founded the *Princeton
Tory*, a conservative, Reaganite-Thatcherite student journal of the sort that
was being established at many American universities at the time. An encounter with the Jewish Defence League's Meir Kahane inspired Hazony and a
handful of his friends to return to the faith in which they had been raised.
After completing his doctorate at Rutgers, Hazony joined several of this
same group in Israel, where he served as an advisor to Benjamin Netanyahu,
administered a think-tank and lived in a settlement across the Green Line
until the outbreak of the Second Intifada occasioned a move to Jerusalem.
Hazony quickly found himself implacably opposed to prevailing opinion in
Israeli intellectual circles: the result, a fierce critique of the 'post-Zionism',
avowed and tacit, of the country's elite in his book *The Jewish State* (2000),
announced him as a leading intellectual figure of Jewish conservatism.

In *The Virtue of Nationalism*, Hazony's project is ambitious: wielding two
ideal types, the nation and the empire, he proposes to vindicate the former.
Following his mentor Steven Grosby, he asserts that modern nations in fact
represent a revival of the ancient form of political order exhibited by the
ancient Jewish nation, or people. The independent rule of the Jewish people

over themselves was established in fact 'under the Seleucids', and the theory that a world of limited, self-governing nations is preferable was propounded in the Old Testament, with its descriptions of the survival of the Jewish nation against Egyptian and Babylonian empire. Hazony's definition of the nation is drawn from Deuteronomy: 'The political aspiration of the prophets of Israel', he writes, 'is not empire but a free and unified nation living in justice and peace amid other free nations'.

This nationalism is to be distinguished from imperialism, which promises peace through the unification of all mankind under a single regime. Christianity is the prototypical imperial ideology, but a paradoxical one, since it contains within it a seed of nationalism in the form of the Hebrew scriptures. Hazony sketches a history of nationalism in eclipses and revivals: during the long centuries which followed the conquests of Titus, the national principle lay dormant as empires rose and fell, all until the Reformation—with its attention to the Old Testament—unleashed it once more. The Thirty Years' War pitted Catholic champions of universal empire against Protestant nationalists, with the latter emerging victorious. The new Protestant order rested on two principles, revived from the Old Testament: first, a 'moral minimum' needed for government to be considered legitimate, requiring the ruler to obey the pre-existing laws of the realm; and second, the notion that it was rightful for those nations strong enough to win their independence to maintain it. Still, imperialism has proven as resilient as nationalism, with the post-Westphalian period witnessing first a Napoleonic bid for empire in the nineteenth century and, in the twentieth, twin bids by Nazism and communism. Hazony is firm in classifying Nazi Germany as an imperialist rather than nationalist force: 'Hitler', he writes with the utmost confidence, 'was no advocate of nationalism'.

The Second World War, Hazony maintains, did not put an end to empire but was rather the occasion of the defection to the imperial side by a previously stalwart nationalist force, the United States. American imperialism more often goes by other names—the 'liberal international order', the 'rules-based order', the 'indispensable nation'—but Hazony is contemptuous of such 'murky newspeak'. The criticism extends to the European Union, whose similar deployment of euphemism ('pooled sovereignty', 'ever closer union') is mere window-dressing for an imperial project in the German or Catholic tradition. The appearance of the term 'subsidiarity' in EU law does not escape notice. Yet the EU is not an empire so much as an empire-in-waiting: Europe remains under American rule, with the EU as Washington's 'protectorate'. It will not be until American troops leave Europe that the bloc's imperial ambitions will be actualized in the form of German dominance of the European continent. Hazony applauds the 'new nationalism' of Reagan and Thatcher, as well as the recent Anglo-American rebellion from empire—for the US, retreat from its role as liberal imperialist; for the UK, withdrawal from the European Union.

Hazony then proposes to show how nations, ancient and modern, arise organically through the development of bonds of loyalty between families, 'clans' and 'tribes'. Acknowledging the anachronism of these Biblical terms, Hazony insists they remain applicable today. The nation comes about when a number of tribes agree to join for their mutual security and protection against outsiders. The result is the birth of impersonal justice along fixed standards: the 'rule of law'. But the underlying tribal structure does not disappear, nor do the ties of loyalty and the cultural practices it fixes in place. Here is Hazony's implicit rebuke of Benedict Anderson: the nation is not an imagined community per se, rather a coalition of smaller communities which are not imagined but natural. It is a midpoint between the insecurity and personalized justice of the tribe and the homogenizing uniformity of empire. If nationalists are tribesmen compared to cosmopolitans, they are cosmopolitans compared to tribesmen.

While Hazony maintains these tribal roots of the nation are not based entirely on ties of blood—he considers the matter settled after citing the example of Ruth the Moabite—he rejects two flavours of civic nationalism, Habermasian 'constitutional patriotism' and the ambient American notion of the 'creedal' or 'propositional' nation. (He does not cite Renan but seems no less hostile to French-style voluntarist notions of a nationalism based in a *plébiscite de tous les jours*.) Such notions deny the historically and culturally specific origin of the nation, in America's case arising from English common law and Old Testament-inspired Protestantism. Jefferson's supposed liberal universalism and revolutionary fervour is excoriated while Hamilton is recast as a Tory. America's immigrants, such as its Catholics, must be considered additional 'tribes' adopted into the larger family. Hazony stops short of unequivocal endorsement of a right to national independence. Demanding 'parsimony' in his order of national states and citing logistical constraints, Hazony regretfully informs the reader that many groups that perhaps might like to become nations must remain mere tribes in a larger national body. He attacks European colonialism for drawing up the borders of what are now postcolonial states without regard for national division, making the development of free national states through consent of tribal leaders nearly impossible. This is the only moment in the book in which an area of the world beyond Europe, the United States and Israel comes into view.

Hazony pairs his ideal types with rival epistemologies: nationalists, he says, are generally empiricists, while imperialists are rationalists. Drawing upon his 2017 essay in *American Affairs* with confrère Ofir Haivry, Hazony contrasts the tradition of ancient-constitutionalist English thinkers (John

Fortescue, John Selden, Edward Coke—roughly the subject of J. G. A. Pocock's 1957 monograph *The Ancient Constitution and the Feudal Law*) with a liberal tradition that stretches from Locke through Rousseau and Kant to Hayek, Mises and Rawls. The former he praises, Selden especially because of his study of Talmudic law, and terms historical empiricists. These thinkers recognize the contingent and specific character of the uniquely virtuous English political system, as do their conservative successors, most significantly Burke. Locke, too, praised the English constitution but committed the error of attempting to derive it from the reasoned consent of individuals by means of a state-of-nature argument. The universalizing tendency of this move opened the way for liberal imperialism, from the French Revolution to 'democracy promotion' in the Middle East, as Locke's successors sought to impose English-style government on societies plainly unfit for it, or even to collapse the world's nations into a single federation. Moreover, liberal theory threatens the ties of 'tribal' loyalty on which nations depend because it does not recognize them and instead imagines all associations to derive from rational, self-interested individual consent, as if the nation were a mere business partnership.

The last section, 'Anti-Nationalism and Hate', argues that while some nationalists do become antagonistic towards outsiders, they are largely peaceful and virtuous, and this tendency toward violence is if anything more pronounced among imperialist universalists of any stripe. While the archetypal example is Christian anti-Semitism, the chapter consists in large part of a meditation on anti-Zionism in the West. Hazony suggests that European opinion holds his country, Israel, to a different standard from surrounding Arab countries because the Israelis are erstwhile Europeans. In the logic of the Kantian progression from barbarism through nationalism into cosmopolitanism, the Israelis have regressed from the third stage to the second, and for this must be blamed. The state of Israel, Hazony polemically insists, is either 'Auschwitz' or 'not Auschwitz'. To Israelis, it represents the political power which will prevent them from relying on the goodwill of other nations for their survival—that is, the predicament which generated Auschwitz. To European critics, its Law of Return and its constitution as an explicitly Jewish state represent the primitive nationalism which generated Auschwitz. The choice between these two alternatives is analogous to the overarching choice presented by the book, between nation and empire.

How should *The Virtue of Nationalism* be assessed? It may be simplest to start with the historical chapters. Hazony's founding of nationalism on the strictures of Deuteronomy gives him *carte blanche* to ignore the modern literature on the subject; Gellner, Kedourie, Benedict Anderson are listed in a single footnote. The influence of the Old Testament on Protestantism is emphasized uncritically: the only interpretation of the Bible suggested to be less than purely faithful and accurate is that of Locke. As his several citations of Kissinger's *World Order* indicate, Hazony's notions about the significance of the Thirty Years' War are indebted to notions of 'Westphalian sovereignty' which, regardless of the efforts of Stephen Krasner and others, remain common in the American field of international-relations theory, despite lacking a firm basis in the history of the period. Catholic France is placed on the Protestant-nationalist side without explanation, and the imperialistic tendencies of Hazony's infant national states (Britain, France, the Netherlands)—already in evidence at the time, from Ireland to the Indian Ocean—go unmentioned. Neither is Hazony consistent in his own assessment. The treaties which concluded the Thirty Years' War, he writes, 're-founded the entire political order'. There is an endnote appended to this sentence, which begins: 'The three Westphalia treaties do not announce a new political order'.

In a review of Hazony's *The Jewish State*, Mark Lilla noted that the author's posture was not a recognizably Israeli one but rather that of 'the American counter-intellectual', that is, someone of neoconservative persuasion who engages not so much in intellectual activity *per se* as in the 'battle of ideas' with the goal of restoring, or defending, a previous order. Unlike his predecessors, Irving Kristol and others, Hazony had become a counter-intellectual without ever having been an intellectual. They had been canny generals in the 'battle of ideas'; Hazony was a mere foot-soldier. In his earlier book these shortcomings were compensated by a genuine talent for excoriation and stirring personal appeal, but here Hazony must be a theorist, a less than ideal task for a man of his capacities. His handful of attempts to set down an aphorism illustrate the point. According to Hazony, 'An iron law governing the operation of human reason is this: Whatever is assumed without argument comes to be regarded as self-evident'. This is to say that whatever is regarded as self-evident comes to be regarded as self-evident.

Hazony's reading of the Old Testament as a programme for a world of peaceful sovereign nations is not a natural one: for each passage in Deuteronomy containing a divine warning against the Israelites' trespassing against other peoples, there is at least one other containing a divine promise to 'dispossess nations greater and mightier than you', to give the Israelites 'their land in estate' (4:38), to have them 'dwell in their towns and in their houses' (19:1–2), to smash their altars and 'cultic pillars' (7:5). These acts, not those of a peaceful, limited nation, are justified in the case of the Israelites because they are divinely ordained; but were the parties to switch roles, the invaders would be divinely punished. It is accordingly difficult to read the text as suggesting a normative theory of international relations which applies the same set of rules to all nations. Hazony's single-mindedly political reading of the Old Testament displays noticeably less concern with religious themes as such than the work of the 'atheist' Rousseau. It is reminiscent of Hazony's earlier monograph on the philosophy of Hebrew scripture, which is full of simple analogies with Greek philosophy and marked by a tendency to abstract away from the central assertion of Israel's chosenness. Hazony's Biblical-political category of 'tribes and clans', as an attempt to give the nation-state a natural rather than artificial character by emphasizing intermediate bodies between individual and state, has a certain Tocquevillian charm. But it is one thing to suggest the existence of a permanent set of contours in politics, and another to project an idea of primitive social structures—pertaining to an agrarian kingdom of a few hundred thousand inhabitants—directly onto modern societies and expect to produce a theory with explanatory force.

What of Hazony's critique of classical liberal theory? He proposes a 'philosophy of political order' which he takes to be prior to Greek 'philosophy of government' and free of the fallacies of liberal theory. 'The enduring weakness of political philosophy descended from Hobbes and Locke', Hazony insists, is the centrality given to the 'calculations of consenting individuals'. Yet his own account begins with the individual. Individuals, he says, may decide to join institutions, like tribes or clans (apparently already in existence, although he claims to show how they originate). Three possible reasons may impel them to the choice: fear, hope for advantage, or—and in the best case—when they 'see the interests and aims of the institution as their own'. That is to say, if one chooses an institution on the grounds that its interests are judged identical to one's own interests, the decision is made from self-interest. The 'loyalty' to the collective to which Hazony offers such fulsome praise arises, according to him, out of rational, self-interested individual consent no less than Locke's does. He has managed nothing more than the introduction of an intermediate step into the formation of the state by means of the social contract—that is all that his 'tribes and clans' amount to. Hazony calls the free but unstable condition of the world before the formation of the nation 'anarchy', but he would be better advised to call it what it is: the Lockean state of nature, in which the punishment of crimes is not yet depersonalized. As if this is not enough, Hazony describes explicitly as a social contract the formation of the state by voluntary consent of 'tribal' leaders. Eradicating any doubt that he is unaware of how short a distance he has travelled in the course of his critique of liberal theory, Hazony blithely asks the reader to note how 'distant' his account is 'from the founding of the state as described in the theories of Hobbes or Locke'.

No such theory is presented to explain the origin of empire. Hazony suggests that empires preach sympathy with mankind, but in fact depend on an internal loyalty in opposition to the other, to the unconverted. (Hazony's nations depend too, he says, on loyalty formed in opposition to the other.)

He also suggests that all empires are constituted to favour the original nation from which they grew. The implicit notion that an empire is a nation gone wrong, a nation that has overthrown its boundaries, is a greater threat to Hazony's system than he seems to recognize: it hints that his injunction to nations not to interfere in other nations' affairs is not self-enforcing. The dismissal of the city-state—incompatible with his framework—and its thought leaves him unable to address the argument of Machiavelli, that the only truly reliable means of security for states is to seek *grandezza*. For the same reason Hazony has little to say about the internal organization of 'national states', that is, regime type. To avoid the term 'democracy' he engages in Millian hand-waving: a 'free state' is one where 'the cooperation of the ruled is given to the government voluntarily'. Here lies a key difference between Hazony's critique of liberal imperialism and left critiques which emphasize notions of democratic self-determination.

The segment of Hazony's readership most equipped to criticize him on these grounds are the followers of Leo Strauss, but they are prohibited from doing so openly by the rules of their sect, since Hazony defends an order they too wish to preserve. (The tone of the review in the *Claremont Review*, the house journal of West Coast Straussianism, is indicative.) It is worth considering what their tacit objections are likely to be. Straussians are known for combining outward defence of the nation and its laws with an inward, self-consciously philosophical contempt for such things, supposedly derived from Plato's scorn for Athenian democracy. Hazony's work, which has none of the remove they cultivate, thus necessarily seems reflexive and unphilosophical. It does not pose 'the question of the best regime'; it does not inquire whether the traditions to be defended are good ones, nor whether the 'family, clan or tribe' deserves the loyalty it demands. It is based, as they say, on opinion rather than knowledge. They are too cautious to assert that liberalism and communism are comparable—although they believe that they are—and they are too careful readers of Machiavelli and Rousseau to suppose, as Hazony does, that a unified people must exist before there can be laws and a state to govern them. To assert this is to misunderstand the role of the lawgiver, which is to create a people at the same time as he frames their laws. Moses had an Egyptian name, but his text disguises this fact. (This posture is in fact more compatible than Hazony's with that of Gellner and Anderson.)

Hazony rejects the Straussian reading of Rousseau in a footnote, confirming the disagreement, and also bringing to mind that it is a shame he does not seem to have paid attention to his Rousseau—if he had, he may have recognized an influence on his anti-cosmopolitan plea for peace among nations, noted also by Lilla. Straussians take issue with Hazony's claim that the material collected in the Hebrew Bible contains the 'first great works' of the 'Western political tradition': for the Straussians this title must go to the dialogues of Plato. Even if the texts of the Hebrew Bible were to precede chronologically the texts of Greek antiquity (a subject of debate) they are genealogically second and philosophically secondary.

The reaction of the Straussians reminds us that Hazony's book was addressed to an American conservative intellectual establishment divided in the wake of the election of Donald Trump. After 2016, with large swathes of that establishment committed to a critical stance towards the President, the way had been opened for an insurgent new dispensation that might take inspiration from aspects of the Trump phenomenon with or without the man himself. West Coast Straussians like Michael Anton, early converts, saw Trump as a chance to wrest back control from progressive hijackers of the American ship of state. In the same period, a new policy journal, *American Affairs*, began to publish bold proposals for government agencies, showcasing the potential of an American right liberated from the straitjacket of free trade and the free market. Especially on the religious right—where there was always some tension with the 'fusionist' position—a new temperament was emerging: proudly nationalistic, critical of foreign wars yet hawkish on China, deeply resentful of conservative compromise on 'social issues' like abortion and gay rights, critical of classical liberal theory, agnostic on the free market. It was a Catholic who was to produce the first notable work of the new movement, which now began to be called 'post-liberal'. Notre Dame professor Patrick Deneen took on the role of a cynical Tocqueville in *Why Liberalism Failed* (2016), albeit without Tocqueville's power of sociological insight. The atomization of American society and the ravages of deindustrialization were, he wrote, foreordained by the nation's liberal founding. The book was criticized by the free-market right and praised by the religious right: a chasm yawned between *National Review*, the venerable fusionist organ, and *First Things*, the pugilistic flagship magazine of the religious right. In this context, Hazony and his book represented something of an olive branch. He purported to criticize Locke but, as we have seen, without actually departing from him; instead of rejecting the American founding he claimed merely to prefer Hamilton to Jefferson. The free market was affirmed but not dogmatically (the old neoconservative position, Kristol's 'two cheers'). The 'post-liberal' movement had challenged American conservatism from the perspective of the right: Hazony meant only to re-establish a robust 'national conservatism'.

As such Hazony's book found a friendly reception both in Deneen's orbit and also in *National Review*. Only Samuel Goldman sounded a decidedly contrary note in *Modern Age*. Ignored by most of the liberal press, with the exception of *New York* magazine's in-house conservative and the *New Republic*, it was awarded 'Conservative Book of the Year' in 2019 and has become required reading in right-of-centre circles. Hazony's status as an American-educated Israeli was also significant in the reception of his book, as Israel's valence on the American right is in flux. Many of its erstwhile 'paleo-conservative' critics have come to believe that the country possesses the qualities they find lacking in American society: right-wing youth, high birth-rates, religious displays welcome in the 'public square', a strong sense of national purpose. Israel alone has what every country must have to survive: 'God and enemies'. Who better to trust on the subject of nationalism than a citizen of the nation *par excellence*? Hazony was in the enviable position of being, from his vantage point in Jerusalem, less bound to respect the customary sacred cows of the US right, yet possessed of a highly secure set of conservative bona fides. Established as a broadly acceptable intellectual standard-bearer for the new dispensation, Hazony now began to organize on its behalf. He was already a serial intellectual entrepreneur. Besides his *Princeton Tory* and the Shalem Center, a think-tank which transformed into Israel's first American-style liberal-arts college, there was also *Azure*, a now-defunct magazine; and finally the Herzl Institute, another think-tank. His latest enterprise is the Edmund Burke Foundation, which he conducts in coordination with R. R. Reno, editor of *First Things*, and Christopher DeMuth, a former president of the staunchly neoliberal American Enterprise Institute. These two figures are indicative of some sources of support for the new national conservatism: Catholic intellectuals, who have long held reservations about the relationship between capitalism and social atomization; and veterans of the conservative movement, apparent converts from the free market.

In the past several years Hazony has organized a series of conferences under the 'national conservative' banner. The first of these, convened in the summer of 2019, starred two potential presidential candidates associated with the movement, Missouri senator Josh Hawley and Fox News anchor Tucker Carlson, and attracted a raft of press, notably a treatment by Thomas Meaney in *Harper's*—especially after a speaker, a law professor named Amy Wax, suggested conservatives should not be shy about championing immigration policies that privileged whites. Hazony defended Wax, arguing that her remarks had been misinterpreted. But it should not be concluded that Hazony has no enemies to his right. His distinction between Protestant- and Jewish-aligned nationalism and Catholic-aligned empire is helpful as a heuristic for navigating the arguments among right-wing American 'critics of liberalism'. While Hazony's coterie includes Catholics like Reno, Deneen and J. D. Vance, his book casts the Church as a chief villain, and as such it is not surprising that a more ultramontane faction, the 'integralists', despises him and considers his nationalism to be idolatrous. Their appellation, recalling the French *intégristes*, indicates a type more familiar in

Catholic Europe than in America. Led by a vanguard composed of a blogging Cistercian monk and a Harvard Law professor named Adrian Vermeule, they demand that the temporal power of the state be subordinated to the spiritual power of the Church. Vermeule, a specialist in administrative law, was prior to his conversion an exponent of the 'nudge' theory of Cass Sunstein. This theory, which emphasizes the temptation of man to err and the need for benevolent experts gently to direct him toward his own good, already has a certain Catholic flavour. It is a disposition Vermeule has smoothly integrated, so to speak, into his new faith, adeptly mixing a Maistrean sense of liberalism as *felix culpa* with a tacit Weberianism that considers the teaching of the Church as a 'value' which may be inserted like any other into the bureaucratic equation: sacraments instead of soda taxes. The 'administrative state'—the executive-branch agencies with broad powers of statutory interpretation, otherwise the bugbear of US conservatives—is in Vermeule's eyes a prime target for infiltration by Catholic paladins. Properly harnessed, it can be deployed to open the floodgates to Catholic immigration, ban abortion, pornography and blasphemy, redistribute income and promote the true faith, by the sword if necessary. To secure all this, the Constitution need not be rewritten, only reinterpreted, with the 'general welfare clause' a suitable Trojan horse for Thomism. Soon Vermeule will have the opportunity to see how far this method will take him: at the time of this writing, he is set to receive an appointment to a best-practices committee, the Administrative Conference, within the federal administrative bureaucracy.

A second National Conservatism conference was held in Rome in early February 2020, coinciding auspiciously with the publication of the Italian translation of *The Virtue of Nationalism*—and, less auspiciously, with the first Italian coronavirus cases, a pair of Chinese tourists in a hotel on the Via Cavour (not far from the conference venue). Hazony was seeking to extend his influence to Europe and with his co-organizers had recruited a wide range of right-wing and Eurosceptic figures, among them Marion Maréchal, darling of the French right, and Viktor Orbán, lately the favourite statesman of American national conservatives. The conference title—'Ronald Reagan, John Paul II, and the Freedom of Nations'—suggested Hazony's attempt to reframe, if slightly, the familiar Cold War refrains in his own language of nationalism and imperialism. The Soviets had been defeated by Reagan and Thatcher so that the nations of Europe could be free, but now their freedom was menaced once more by the European Union. There was also an attempt to make amends with the Catholics, as suggested by the conference's location and dedication; on their behalf Hazony now praised the Church as a bulwark against Soviet imperialism.

But the Cold War has lost much of its power as a unifying force on the right, and the speakers could not agree on Hazony's narrative. Orbán refused to praise either the Pope (Orbán is a Calvinist) or Margaret Thatcher (they had had some disagreement over Yugoslavia), and insisted, unsurprisingly, that Hungary had to chart an independent course within the European Union, rather than leave it. Hazony may still feel himself a Reaganite, but the Reagan Administration veterans sent over from Washington could not join him in denouncing NATO as an imperial project, nor even the European Union, the formation of which they had welcomed at the time. As for the Catholics, the Polish writer and MEP Ryszard Legutko, who is ardently cherished by Vermeule for his book, *The Demon in Democracy* (2016), did not help matters by repeating to the appalled Reaganites the book's thesis that liberal democracy and communism are similar regimes. Meanwhile, the broader agenda of the new national conservatism seemed to fade from view. The first of Hazony's conferences had embraced the adoption of an American 'industrial policy', a clear break from conservative economic orthodoxy, but now Christopher DeMuth, Hazony's co-organizer, complained of the abandonment of 'fiscal restraint' in the US and UK.

To gain purchase, an insurgent movement within American conservatism must have wide appeal, yet not be so ecumenical that it regresses to the mean. Strategic sacrifices from the programme may have to be made. Under Hazony's direction the movement's most intellectually fruitful subject, its economic heterodoxy as explored in the pages of *American Affairs*, may be the first thing to go. Hazony is clearly uninterested in the subject, a fact which his occasional gestures to an inchoate 'economic nationalism' cannot disguise. What will survive this process of *trasformismo*? Hazony cheers on Eurosceptics from a distance but does not seriously desire the withdrawal of US troops from Europe. He certainly does not demand a change in US policy towards his own country. He is not even a perceptible China hawk. The residuum is in large part a familiar and, it must be said, inert set of injunctions about American national self-worth and public displays of religion. The Catholics of the new radical right are more or less to be believed when they say there is nothing for them to cherish in liberal theory or its regime, but the same cannot be said for Hazony. If liberalism had only enemies like him, it would be in no need of friends.

Keir Milburn, *Generation Left*
Polity Press: Cambridge 2019, £9.99, paperback
139 pp, 978 1 5095 3223 0

OLIVER EAGLETON

POLITICAL GENERATIONS

Last December, YouGov analysis of the 2019 UK general election results found, to nobody's surprise, that 'age is still the biggest dividing line in British politics'. Labour had a 43-point advantage with the under-25s, while the Tories led by 47 points among the over-65s. Likelihood of voting Conservative increased by 9 per cent for every decade of life. This disparity was just as pronounced during the 2017 election—when the gap in voting intentions between the youngest and oldest grew to a cavernous 97 per cent—and the EU referendum, which saw retirees back Leave in overwhelming numbers. Yet the generational fault-line now taken for granted by the commentariat has opened up rapidly. Just ten years ago, support for the main parties was roughly equal among 18–24 year-olds.

This sudden polarization—which has informed several progressive insurgencies since the financial crash: not just Corbyn's Labour, but Podemos, Syriza, Mélenchon, Sanders—is the subject of Keir Milburn's *Generation Left*: a concise intervention on the relationship between age and class, pooling the theoretical resources of Mannheim, Tronti and Badiou to identify what generates a generation. Milburn is a lecturer in political economy at the University of Leicester and an active member of Plan C: a diffuse anti-capitalist collective that uses experimental organizing methods to raise consciousness and combat the far-right. He co-hosts the 'Acid Corbynism' podcast on Novara Media, which applies Fisherian *Kulturkritik* to hippyish topics like love, freedom and friendship, and his new book is inflected by this outlook: eclectic in its references, optimistic in its analysis, acutely sensitive to cultural affects.

Milburn begins by dispelling the idea that generations are established solely through demographic trends. The Baby Boomers, he writes, came about through a dramatic rise in birth-rates between 1945 and 1965, yet this bulge was bookended by two events that demography cannot explain: the end of WWII and the introduction of the contraceptive pill, both of which influenced the ideological character of this cohort. Any account of generational formation that neglects these social and technological developments—focusing instead on endogenous population patterns—is therefore incomplete. It is vital to excavate the factors that underpin shifting birth-rates, rather than treating them as given.

Indeed, Baby Boomers are one of the only clear examples of a demographic overhaul coinciding with a distinct cultural identity. Millennials were not created by any correlative population spike, yet their alienation from older age-groups remains akin to what Boomers experienced in the 60s. For Milburn, this confirms Mannheim's thesis—outlined in his 1923 essay, 'The Problem of Generations'—that generations are produced by 'dynamic de-stabilization', or rapid historical change. A new, cohesive age category emerges when, 'as a result of an acceleration in the tempo of social and cultural transformation, basic attitudes must change so quickly that the latent, continuous adaptation and modification of traditional patterns of experience, thought and expression is no longer possible'. This explains why generations rarely conform to the cyclical 20 or 30-year timescales set out by sociologists. In periods of calm, young people inherit the existing worldview. When that stasis is disrupted, they coalesce around a different schema.

This coalescence takes place because the youth respond to transformative historical processes with an 'elasticity of mind'. Their relative lack of experience makes them susceptible to the 'moulding power of new situations', capable of aligning their perspective with altered realities, whereas their parents have built up a 'framework of useable past experience, so that every new experience has its form and its place largely marked out for it in advance'. Mannheim insists that this distinction does not make the young inherently progressive and the old incurably conservative. 'Youth and age ... do not of themselves involve a definite intellectual or practical orientation; they merely initiate certain formal tendencies, the actual manifestations of which will ultimately depend on the prevailing social and cultural context'. Yet when we consider the 2008 financial crisis—and the austerity measures that flowed from it—there are obvious reasons why these tendencies produced a decisive leftward swing among teenagers and twentysomethings.

The bankruptcy of Lehman Brothers, writes Milburn, was an earth-shattering Badiouian Event: 'a moment of sudden and unpredictable change that ruptures society's sense making'. By fracturing the neoliberal symbolic order, it called for the instatement of new Subjects and new Truths—for a political orientation beyond the tired fatalism of the 90s. This was a call that the young, 'lacking a solid interpretive prism formed of past experience', were uniquely capable of answering. It was their responsibility to dismantle the 'entrepreneurial self' which Milburn sees as the linchpin of post-Fordist ideology. The primary objective of the Thatcher–Reagan programme, he argues, was not to push through economic reforms that favoured capital, but to deflate the communalist energies unlocked by the Keynesian settlement and replace them with a model of property-owning individualism. The cultural efflorescence of the 70s reflected an emerging horizon of possibility that was incompatible with capitalism itself. This utopian climate was destroyed by the doctrine of There Is No Alternative, which promoted 'investment in the self' over collective empowerment, as if societal futures had to close so that individual prospects could open. But it is precisely this belief in individual futurity that the Event of '08 belied, exposing major flaws in the system supposed to guarantee a profitable return on self-investment. Over the following years, young people watched their life chances crumble amidst the housing crisis, student loan debt and labour-market precaritization. The result was a transcendence of entrepreneurial ontology.

Milburn describes the 2008 meltdown as a 'passive event': 'something that happened to us' rather than something we participated in. Within six months it had 'disappeared behind the spectre of deficits in government budgets', and the onset of austerity compounded the impression that 'possibilities were closing down'. But while this feeling of disempowerment triggered far-right mobilizations amongst the youth of Eastern Europe, in other countries it yielded to the 'active events' of 2010–11: Occupy Wall Street in the US, the student movement in Britain, anti-austerity demonstrations in Western Europe, revolutionary upheavals in the Arab world. Each of these constituted a 'moment of excess' in which street-level activism allowed subjectivities to form outside of neoliberal logic. Despite the geographical and political differences between such moments, they shared a striking number of organizational forms, including democratic assemblies and consensus-based decision-making: a commonality that, for Milburn, speaks to a unified process of generational construction, developing common techniques in response to common problems.

His distinction between passive and active events makes effective use of Tronti's class composition theory. The crisis of 2008 was 'passive' because it revealed what Tronti called the 'technical composition' of the working class—their objective circumstances, defined by diminishing prospects and burgeoning debt. The frenetic activity of 2011, on the other hand, gave the proletariat its 'political composition': the methods and modalities evolved through struggle to overcome those circumstances. Age became 'one of the key modalities through which class is lived' because it was central to these post-crash insurrections, in which the youth—shaken out of their complacency by the Event—escaped the neoliberal thought-world still populated by their elders.

Although these moments of excess proved ephemeral, they created a politicized generational unit that 'stayed internally highly networked', and regrouped in 2014–16 to initiate 'the electoral turn'. Milburn surveys the rise (and, usually, fall) of party-political movements spearheaded by Generation Left in Greece, Spain, the US and the UK, suggesting—with a nod to the autonomist tradition—that the state suppression of the 2011 uprisings was what catalysed this switch from extra-parliamentary activism to electoral agitation. If Occupy could not withstand the power of the state, then the state itself had to be seized. Yet this project suffered from three intractable problems: it failed to form a viable electoral coalition with older generations; it was forced to work through institutions which sapped the participative spirit of 2011; and it remained vulnerable to a counter-attack by the forces of capital—the media and banking sectors in particular.

For Milburn, such barriers can only be surmounted when Generation Left redoubles its attempt to forge an anti-capitalist ethic which could radiate to older age brackets. The breakdown of entrepreneurial selfhood places young people in a 'politically ambiguous' position. 'When the common sense of a society stops making sense but change through collective action seems out of reach, people must create ad hoc subjectivities from the material to hand'. This threatens to entrench the isolation instilled by neoliberalism. Disaffected with the dominant order, yet lacking a countercultural alternative, the youth may retreat into narcissistic self-pathologization, adopting psychotherapeutic discourses to create individual meanings in lieu of collective narratives. Milburn therefore calls for a 'reinvention of adulthood' that would complete Generation Left's political composition by producing a stable, post-neoliberal subjectivity. The present conception of grown-upness, he claims, is closely linked to private property. Since the 1980s, adulthood has centred on ownership, of oneself and one's home. Hence, the immediate task is to turn Generation Rent's dispossession into a positive, 'commons-based' mode of living. 'The most vital plank of any programme must be the massive expansion of cooperative housing and the spread of intergenerational co-housing'. There is no need to wait for a left government to take these steps: 'Powerful solidarity networks and renters' unions, in which participants pledge to back each other up over disputes with landlords and companies, can be built now'. The revolution in housing must be accompanied by the construction of a digital commons—one that harnesses the 'sociality, self-expression, collective creation and autonomy' permeating social media, yet wrests these energies away from predatory tech-giants. Finally, 'collective practices of care' must be developed to repair the damage done by unconstrained capital and inculcate forms of labour that at least partially elude monetization, creating a shadow economy at odds with the 'sociopathy of neoliberalism'. Through these solidaristic methods, Generation Left can increase its ability to act as a cohesive unit, and recalibrate adulthood to break with exploitation.

Milburn's confidence that the radical youth could hegemonize the older generations—or at least 'peel away a decisive minority' of their members— echoes Mannheim's assertion that a generational 'entelechy' can acquire enough force to represent the culture as a whole. Yet before the spirit of an age-group can become the spirit of the age, another process of hegemonization must take place; according to Mannheim, a self-conscious vanguard within the generation must impress its values upon a majority of its peers. Only when this forward-thinking faction has captured its 'generational location' can its views seep into society at large. A generation must be hegemonized by its internal vanguard before it can become a vanguard in itself. On the surface, voting patterns and opinion polls seem to reflect Milburn's faith that this first stage of hegemony has been achieved: the under-25s are likely to support left parties and self-describe as socialists. But a closer look at the data makes one doubt whether the vanguard's principles—say, the democratic socialism of Momentum or the DSA—have maintained their coherence among the broader swathes of Generation Left. For instance, a recent Gallup poll showed that while nearly 50 per cent of American millennials have a favourable image of 'socialism', almost as many have a positive view of 'big business', and 83 per cent look approvingly on 'free enterprise'. When questioned on specific issues, this cohort's 'elasticity of mind' sometimes sounds like fickleness. In Britain, a similar degree of ideological disorientation is evident in Generation Left's uncritical endorsement of the EU (far more popular with young voters than Corbyn's party), its disappointing turnout rate in 2019 (only 47 per cent), and its election of Keir Starmer as Labour leader.

So, if committed socialists are a sizeable faction within Generation Left rather than its overriding hegemon, what does this mean for Milburn's account of the current generational divide? His exaggeration of Generation Left's radical credentials is partly down to the conditions under which he was writing, before Corbynism capsized in December. But it is also a symptom of the book's uneasy attempt to reconcile Badiou and Tronti. As we have seen, the Trontian categories of 'technical composition' and 'political composition' are mapped onto the 'passive event' of 2008 and the 'active event' of 2011. The first exposed systemic injustice, the second emboldened the young to confront it. Yet this splitting of the Event into discrete parts is a departure from Badiou, for whom the notion of a 'passive event' would be oxymoronic. In Badiou's theory, Events create an instant expansion of political possibility by puncturing the 'state', or illusory consistency of the social world; they are

R
E
V
I
E
W
S

site-specific, rooted in a particular locality; they become Events when their participants designate them as such; and they carry a 'maximal intensity of appearance', asserting their presence through spectacle. It is hard to see how any of this applies to 2008, which was mostly invisible (occurring in abstract rather than concrete space), which had no mass participation, and which prompted an immediate foreclosure of possibility, allowing the state to reassert itself through the imposition of austerity.

In one way it is incidental whether the financial crash conforms to this exact definition: it does not affect the basic point that many young people moved leftward in its wake. But if we accept that 2008 was not an Event proper, then we will be better placed to understand why Milburn's favoured generation has not yet reached a vanguardist position. For some, the galvanizing force of 2011 may have changed passivity into activity, disenchantment into engagement. But for many, the process of politicization has remained 'passive', in the sense that it has hinged on everyday frustrations—sky-high rent, gig economy work—which make the statements of Corbyn and Sanders particularly resonant. This process, in which mounting exasperation with one's circumstances causes one to vote for the politician who empathizes with them, can be significant on a personal and electoral level; but it is a far cry from Badiou's narrative of political subject-formation, in which a sudden and singular happening gives rise to a robust oppositional ideology, which then becomes an 'object of faith' for those who experienced the Event, and those who recognize the regime of Truth that it inaugurated.

This is, if you like, a problem with Generation Left's political composition—the predominance of passive events has created 'ad hoc' and 'ambiguous' subjectivities, rather than revolutionary and Evental ones. But there is also an issue with its technical composition. Although Milburn is adept at showing how 'political generations are intimately entwined with the dynamics of class struggle', he overlooks the instability of Generation Left's class coalition. This is, after all, a category that includes the offspring of bankers and cleaners, schoolteachers and stockbrokers. It is riven with inequality. Yet its distinct elements are more or less politically aligned because even affluent 21-year-olds experience economic pressures, like rent and debt, that expose the sham of neoliberal subjecthood. Millennials can therefore be described as a 'populist' grouping, according to the definition set out by Michael Denning in NLR 122: an alliance of disparate social forces which come together around 'livelihood struggles', or non-wage-based forms of exploitation. Livelihood struggles have a socially equalizing effect that enables the political unification of structurally antagonistic actors. But how long this unity will last is indeterminate. For Generation Left, it could be unravelled by political changes that re-orient struggle away from these 'subordinate' forms, or by the unequal distribution of inherited wealth, which will propel some young people onto the property ladder while others continue renting.

By neglecting these contingencies, Milburn risks replacing class politics with progressivism. His homogeneous depiction of Generation Left as a culturally advanced agent elides the complexities of its material composition. Socio-economic data on this age-group is supplanted by the murkier discourse of subjectivity. As such, he is more interested in honing a certain cultural identity (through experiments in communal living), than building cross-generational solidarity among proletarianized classes. This is not to say that Milburn's inspiring programme for a new 'commons' should be dismissed. On the contrary, to understand Generation Left as an unstable populist coalition increases the urgency of this project. For if the material basis of its radicalism remains fragile, that is all the more reason to engender new material realities—through the proliferation of cooperatives and care-work. If its egalitarianism is still conjectural, that should encourage us to embed it in lived experience, via community organizing and participatory democracy. Such street-level exercises could become the concrete embodiment of Generation Left's abstract commitment. They could generate a new symbolic order without the intervention of a messianic Event. Yet they should always be coupled with a class consciousness that grasps the volatility of generational politics—the potential for its populist reason to erode—and reaches out to older age-groups, not by inviting them into our 'post-capitalist' world, but by stressing the common depredations of the world we all inhabit.